RACING TACTICS FOR CYCLISTS

RACING TACTICS FOR CYCLISTS

THOMAS PREHN

WITH CHARLES PELKEY

Boulder, Colorado

Racing Tactics for Cyclists
© 2004 Thomas Prehn

Printed in the United States of America.

10 9 8 7 6 5

Distributed in the United States and Canada by Publishers Group West.

International Standard Book Number: 1-931382-30-1

Library of Congress Cataloging-in-Publication Data

Prehn, Thomas.
    Racing tactics for cyclists / Thomas Prehn, with Charles Pelkey.
        p. cm.
    Includes index.
    ISBN 1-931382-30-1 (pbk. : alk. paper)
        1. Bicycle racing. I. Pelkey, Charles. II. Title.
GV1049.P64 2004
796.6'2—dc22   2004004530

VeloPress®
1830 North 55th Street
Boulder, Colorado 80301–2700 USA
303/440-0601 • Fax 303/444-6788 • E-mail velopress@insideinc.com

To purchase additional copies of this book or other VeloPress® books, call 800/234-8356 or visit us on the Web at velopress.com.

Cover photo by Graham Watson.
Cover design by Miguel Santana and Liz Jones.
Interior design and composition by Liz Jones.

CONTENTS

FOREWORD

To say I was more than a little miffed when Thomas Prehn won the 156-mile USPRO Championship in 1986 would be something of an understatement.

Weren't we, the 7-Eleven squad, simply the best team with the strongest riders sitting on the Philadelphia start line that hot June morning? Weren't we *supposed* to have one of our own crossing the finish line with arms raised in triumph? I know that I was one who thought so. But Thomas didn't agree and with his textbook use of smart tactics he adroitly "schooled" us.

Through the first 125 miles, I felt good about our chances. The race had played out in our favor—all of team 7-Eleven's top riders were still in the bunch as the infamous Manayunk Wall, the enervating heat, and distance whittled the pack down. But in road racing, unlike most other forms of endurance sport, while it's true that the strongest usually survive, it doesn't mean they always win. Thomas, ever the master tactician, played it perfectly. He carefully shepherded his energy throughout the long day. He kept himself off our radar, so to speak, by riding discreetly in the early part of the race. He was active at the front but not *too* active.

His sublime move was then perfectly timed, coinciding not with the hardest part of the course, but the point where we were recovering. He'd "read" the race perfectly, too, jumping free when all eyes were on the so-called favorites. Once clear, he joined forces with a strong Danish rider, and they put their hard training to use, working to gain time on us, the chasers. On the line, Thomas won the two-up sprint and a well-deserved victory, not to mention the title of USPRO Champion. Outsmarted and outridden, I pedaled slowly back to the hotel, reflecting on what went wrong, feeling more than a little envious, very tired . . . and angry. In the biggest domestic event of the season, in front of tens of thousands of spectators, Thomas proved how using smart tactics could humble even the most potent of rivals.

Tactics are what makes racing fun. If it was cut-and-dry and all about who was fittest, then it would simply be a matter of having the best genes and training well. Bike racing, however, is more interesting because it's not so basic. Sure, it helps to be born a Lance or a Greg or a Dede, but lacking their innate engines, many lesser-gifted riders have achieved outstanding results. And if it was only about the ability to train hard, then this would not have been the case. Cycling is also very much about utilizing good technique and having a strong tactical sense—having "race smarts," as they say.

Most of what's written these days about improving cycling performance has to do with training—strengthening the motor, understanding heart rate, wattage output, cadence, and so on. Yes, of course, these are all important, but only to a point. The developing racer will progress more rapidly by focusing on efficiency than on wattage. Efficiency is defined as the ability to do something well or achieve the desired result without wasted energy.

Good tactics are the best example of that sort of efficiency; where you sit in the pack, how to ride a pace line properly, when to pull through, how hard you pull, when to sit out, how to set up for a sprint . . . the list goes on and on. The more tactically savvy the rider, the more *efficient* that rider.

Ultimately, this will be the rider best able to put his or her training to good use, as well as the rider most likely to achieve consistently good results—whether on the local Saturday hammerfest or at the national or international level.

Race smarts can tip the balance in favor of a "weaker" rider, even when there's a huge difference in fitness levels. Several years ago, my best friend and former teammate Ron Kiefel went to Arizona with me for the annual Tour de Tucson. This event, a 111-mile charity ride, is mainly for the masses but it's a categorized pro race too. So Ron and I showed up to support the charity, and although our racing careers were long over, we were put right on the front row, next to the Saturn guys, the Shaklee team, and the Mercury riders. Now Ron hadn't touched a bike in a month and was looking pretty conspicuous—feeling out of shape and out of place. Still, when the gun went off, just as in the glory days, Ron went out with the pros. The course looped the city of Tucson and was just flat enough that by following the right wheels, knowing when to hold back and when to close the gaps, he managed to hang in with the diminishing lead pack. And through the crosswind stretch, where Steve Hegg put everyone in the gutter, ripping along in his 53–11 and blowing the pack to bits, Ron stayed on, riding so close to Hegg that they looked like they were riding a tandem. He owned that extra inch of road to the side that no one else would or *could* ride, getting just enough draft to hang on.

Finally, when the lead group was down to just eight, Ron scored the moral victory when Hegg turned around and indignantly shouted "unbelievable—no way that Kiefel's still here!" While many other well-known riders had been dropped, Ron had used his tactical mastery to not only ride with but to get rid of guys far above his fitness level.

When I mentioned Thomas Prehn's "textbook" tactics in winning his USPRO title, I failed to say that at the time, no such textbook existed. Well, now it does! Read his guide to strategy, enjoy the stories, reflect on and reread this book again and again. It is packed full of good advice for riders at all levels.

And then go out and poach the Sunday group ride and rip their legs off!

Davis Phinney
January 2004

PREFACE
Tactics for Everyone

Many years ago, I was a guest speaker at a five-day national developmental clinic for coaches put on by the coaching staff of the U.S. Cycling Federation. By the time the 2-hour segment devoted to tactics got under way, we only had 90 minutes.

I was writing a few notes when the national coach started the lecture. I don't remember his exact words, but I cringed when I heard him say something like, "Tactics and strategy are only for the top riders."

What?!?!

With all due respect, I disagree fundamentally, principally, and wholeheartedly. What are the other 90 percent supposed to do, roll over and play dead? No!

Well, I think I know what the coach was *trying* to say. When you're a national coach looking at a national class event, about 10 percent of the riders do all of the tactical racing. But tactics and strategy are for everyone to apply at their own level. It's going to be tough for a good local rider to mount successful counterattacks or to launch a strong lead-out against a strong and coordinated team. But if those riders understand the tactical side of the race, they stand a much better chance. Even if it doesn't work, the effort is worth something. Win or lose, you will almost always have learned a lesson or two in the process.

A strong grasp of the tactical allows a rider to go beyond his or her physical ability. It's not always the strongest rider who wins but the *smartest*. Even if we're not talking about winning through calculated maneuvers, proper positioning in the pack, and expending energy at the right time, tactics can mean the difference between finishing in the pack and finding yourself off the back. To a national coach, that may not mean anything, but to a racer struggling with stiff competition, it can mean a lot.

The 90 minutes flew by and it seemed as though we hardly covered anything of substance. There were a lot of things those development coaches needed to learn and the camp was certainly very beneficial; I just felt bad that tactics were covered so briefly. I guess that is natural. For coaches, athletes, and trainers who deal with physical efforts—muscular strength, leg speed, and power—the mental aspect of sport gets only a slight mention.

Tactics are not unlike the psychology of sports. It's amazing but true. If you surveyed top athletes on the difference between winning the really close one or losing it, most would say something along the lines of "It was mental." If you asked how much of your ability to win over the opponent is mental rather than physical, they would probably say almost half! And yet how much time is actually devoted to training the mind, either psychologically or tactically? Little. Precious little. I look forward to sharing much, much more of what I know and what other experts know about all aspects of training and racing—physiology and psychology.

INTRODUCTION
Bicycle Racing: An Exercise of the Body and Mind

In the spring of 1987, I started a technical newsletter dedicated to the racing cyclist. That newsletter, *Pro Form Racing*, was designed to pass on detailed training and tactical information that I had gathered over the course of a fourteen-year racing career. Simply put, I wanted readers to be able to avoid common mistakes, ride better, and race smarter.

It's been gratifying to hear from cyclists over the years who have commented on how the newsletter helped them achieve a particular goal in racing. I have even heard from a few that still have the complete catalog of twenty-five issues. I hope that this book will help accelerate your learning process as well as your bike speed.

If you could condense the principles of this book and my philosophy of training and racing, it would be this: You never stop learning.

It's simple—it's the nature of the sport and the nature of life in general. Things are always in a state of change. Your level of fitness is always changing. The sport is changing. Tactics and races are different, depending on the region of the country, the time of year, and even weather conditions.

Think!

Bicycle racing is a thinking man's sport. From tactics to training schedules, you succeed in this sport only with a *combination* of physical and mental fortitude. When you're in a race, there can be a wealth of data for you to draw upon to gain insight as to what tactics or strategy should be employed. The reason most people don't succeed in extracting this valuable information is because it takes a bit of effort. Most riders are satisfied with the effort they put into pushing the pedals around. It's easy to sit in the pack and not really think about the race.

Plan!

It has often been said that the reason more people don't succeed in life is because they don't plan for their success. In bicycle racing, the same holds true. It's hard to sit down in January and come up with a complete training schedule for the year. It's especially hard because it requires people to commit themselves. It's a lot easier to go along with the status quo and avoid uncharted waters. It's a lot easier to stroll up to a race without any plan or objective and "just see what happens." Usually, it's nothing that happens. There's a world of difference when you plan out a week's training or go into a race with some specific game plan. You create expectations that you hope to achieve.

Act!

I recall one time when I was in a training race and keeping an eye on a team largely made up of young and very talented racers. I wanted to see these guys develop into a solid and successful team. They weren't showing much organization at all and other riders were easily having their way with them. A textbook opportunity came and went with a prime sprint and this team didn't contest it. I made my way through the field and found the team coach to ask him why his guys didn't try simple lead-outs.

"Oh," he replied, "we tried that once and it didn't work."

I was dumbfounded! Imagine the logic. It was like saying, "Oh, we tried to win once but it didn't work, so we won't try that foolishness again."

Few are ever successful at anything the first time. It's from trying and trying again that you find the correct combination.

Whether it's training techniques or racing tactics, make a plan and act on your plan. Sometimes that can be a lot harder to do than you'd expect. It can be hard to resist the temptation to just "go for a ride," as opposed to training. It can be hard to resist the temptation to stay up with a group of your friends on a ride when you *know* you should be resting, riding easy, and recovering.

Finally, *put into cycling what you want to get out of it.* If you want to be a national champion you have to train, act, and think like one. You have to have the dedication and fortitude to win and be the best in the country in your event. It isn't something you turn on inside yourself the last week before the national championship race. The process of winning is one that takes dedication and consistency over months and years.

CHAPTER 1
A Tactical Toolbox

Reading a Race

Do you ever wonder why some racers *always* seem to make it into the winning breaks and others, despite their strength and speed, rarely make it? Sure, some of it has to do with fitness and persistence. Some guys attack so many times that they can't *help* but make it into a winning breakaway now and again.

Over the years, I've watched the best racers in the United States and have seen how the best of the best do it. It's always amazed me how some racers—despite the fact they were world class on the track or in time trials—could never get the hang of tactical racing in a mass-start road race or criterium. Other racers I watched and learned from would sit back 10 or 20 into the field. Through countless attacks and breakaways, they wouldn't budge. Then another group starts off the front of the pack and, in a flash, these "slouchers" would be there, right in the middle of the winning move. Time and time again they would do this in races. Psychic? I'm sure they wish they were but they are not.

These racers aren't sitting back, resting and daydreaming. In fact, they're doing anything but that. They're reading the race: watching, surveying, evaluating everything that's going on around them. They're watching the course. They're watching for the reactions of the pack to each attack and block. They're keeping a running tally of who's off the front, who is blocking, and how well they are blocking. They're watching for signs from key individual racers and keeping tabs on the pulse of the pack as a whole.

Reading a race is a process by which you evaluate all available information and arrive at an educated guess. These educated guesses can help you save energy, help you determine when to attack or where to attack for the best results.

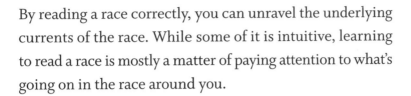

By reading a race correctly, you can unravel the underlying currents of the race. While some of it is intuitive, learning to read a race is mostly a matter of paying attention to what's going on in the race around you.

Assessing the Race before It Happens

You start reading the race before it ever begins. You need to make an assessment of the course and your competitors. What is the course like? What are the noteworthy points about it? Every course has something that will contribute to the outcome of the race—even the most unremarkable courses have something. When you are warming up, always look for potential spots where you can capitalize. Before the race begins, you should consider how the race has been won in the past. This should be a strong indicator for how the race is likely to go this time around.

I recall a flat and fast East Coast circuit race. It was on a perfectly flat circle with no corners. Going into such a race you can figure that, without anything to slow the pack down, the race will be fast and furious from the start. Don't bother to try and jump off the front, unless you just want to warm up or show off to the crowd.

It's likely that most courses will offer more opportunity for decisive race moments than the flat circle. A major climb that splits the field or a particular section on a criterium course that strings out the field will have a bearing on the outcome. As well, the distance of the race plays a significant role in reading the race.

On a criterium circuit, look for points on the course that will slow up the pack or that could be easier for one solo rider to negotiate. Look for places where it will be easy for a strong team to block. Look for areas like a series of corners or a narrow windy road where a breakaway could open up some distance without the pack realizing it. Keep the weather conditions in mind. What effect will wind and rain have on the course, the riders, and yourself?

In a race in Baltimore, Maryland, the course was bound to have a role in determining the outcome. It went from a wide five-lane road at the start/finish to a downhill, off-camber corner and onto a narrow winding roadway. The nature of the rest of the course discouraged breakaways. The narrow road fed into a wide boulevard that climbed gradually up around a bend to the start/finish line. All it would take was one attack by the right folks across the start/finish line with the pack lagging a half lap behind to start the chase. When five top racers sprinted for a prime and opened up a small gap, the pack hesitated, thinking they would slow down after the sprint. Once the riders saw they were clear, they kept their speed up around the off-camber corner and through the narrow section. The pack couldn't negotiate the corner as fast. When they were on the narrow section, three

riders at the front who were unwilling to chase plugged up the road. That was the winning move.

The competitors entered in the race can also be evaluated before the event. For example, is there a strong team that'll probably dominate the race? What individual racers are the strongest, fastest, or tactically the smartest? Historically, how do the key riders or teams ride the race? If there's a team that always does a good job of blocking, you'll want to keep track of their guys off the front. What combinations of riders are going to be dangerous off the front? Who has a strong finish? Who seems to fade?

Does it seem like I'm just posing a lot of questions? That's really all reading a race is about. It's about evaluating all of the information and then trying to use it to determine what's going to happen.

Exercise your judgment. You can sit in the race and day-dream, or you can figure out what's going on so you might ride a more intelligent race.

As the Race Develops

Once you're in the race, you should be concentrating on every-thing that's happening. Who's making the attacks? Is there any-one blocking? Who is it? How is the pack responding? How long is it taking for the pack to chase the attack down? Are the riders off the front a threat? If it's a threatening move, you have to respond even if the pack doesn't. Remember that when a critical move goes, you rarely have but a few seconds to go with it. Otherwise, it's gone.

One of the fundamental methods of reading when the winning breakaway is going to finally go is by keeping track of the duration of each break that takes off the front. Very typically, it takes longer and longer for the pack to chase down the breakaway until finally it doesn't have either the strength or perseverance to do it. At the start of the race, the attacks last for half of a lap and they are made one after another by all sorts of competitors. This is normal, because early on there are a lot of riders who are strong and fresh. As the laps tick by, more and more of the pack start to tire. The attacks later on are only from the better racers, and often it's the same people chasing down these moves. Each time it takes longer for the pack to catch the attacks. Perhaps the breaks stay away a lap or two. Now they're starting to get threatening. Finally, a couple of strong racers go and they have teammates to block. This time it takes five laps to catch them. I'd make sure that I was in the next attack because it's probably the deciding one.

Obviously, the ideal situation is for you to jump only into that final breakaway. Calculating when that will be isn't an exact science. If you have a lot of speed, you can sit near the front of the pack and watch the breakaway start to roll away. At the last minute, when it seems that the pack is not responding—at a distance you know you can still bridge to—jump across to the breakaway. This is the best way to get into a breakaway, but you first have to have that type of speed. Also, your jump can be all that is needed to prod the pack into chasing. You can end up catching the break only a few moments before the rest of the pack catches up.

An obvious thing to watch out for is a strong combination of riders and teams off the front. When I won the USPRO Championships, it was a result of jumping after a potential breakaway with a 7-Eleven and a Danish rider, representing the two strongest teams in the race. There was little question that it was a major threat as the two racers motored down the road at the start of the final big lap of the race. If you keep track of the combinations of riders, you can use your opponent's strengths—namely, his hard-blocking teammates—to *your* advantage.

Most all races come down to the critical moment I've been talking about: "The crunch." When you see it coming, either from an attack, a strong crosswind, or a steep climb, don't hold anything back. Chances are you won't get another opportunity to get back in the running for the race win.

There are other signs you can watch for among your competitors. How do you think they're feeling? If you're riding with competitors of your caliber, ask yourself the question. If you cannot imagine chasing down another breakaway, it's probably a good time to attack. Watch for signs. Look at the way the other riders in the pack are pedaling, how they're breathing. You can even get signs from little things, like how they're eating and drinking. If you notice that they're not eating in a long race or perhaps drinking more than you think necessary, it probably means that they're not feeling well.

You can't just jump into a race and see all of the telltale signs, nor will you know what all of them mean. What's important is that you start with your next race and continue with each race thereafter to sit up and watch what's going on around you. By reading a race correctly, you can far outperform your own physical abilities and those of your competitors. Imagine how much easier it would be and how much fresher you would be if you *only* attacked when the winning breakaway was about to take off. So make those mental notes and after the race, sit down and reevaluate what happened during the race and how and why it happened.

It takes time to learn how to read a race, but I assure you that it will open up a whole new level of racing for you.

Eyeing the Competition

I remember once not so long ago when two of us were out training on the rolling country roads north of Boulder, Colorado. We were riding along steadily when we spotted another rider about a half a mile ahead. We kept our pace up and continued to close until we were within about a quarter of a mile. Then we stopped gaining on the lone rider, so we picked up the pace. Then we picked it up some more.

Still, we weren't closing in on the rider. Now we were mad and a little bit put off by this rider we couldn't catch. From our vantage point, it was obvious the rider we were having trouble catching wasn't even a racer. He had panniers and fenders on his bike! We dropped into a pace line and reeled in the rider. When we finally caught the rider, we saw why he picked up his speed and how he knew he was keeping us at bay. The recreational rider had a mirror on his bike, so he was monitoring our progress and applying the gas to stay ahead of us.

Bike or helmet mirrors aren't the only way, or the best way, to keep track of our competition. We can monitor the situations that are most important—the racers closest to us as we start a sprint or attack, or the progress of a chase group on the breakaway you're in.

Sprint and Attack Situations

In track sprinting, racers have to learn how to ride in front of their competitor, keeping an eye on them and the track at the same time. We know what this looks like. It's a lap and a half to go in the three-lap sprint and the lead rider can't take his eye off the competitor for an instant or they would jump and the race would be over. Once a skilled match sprinter is familiar with a track, it's possible to ride all the way around the track without looking forward. The scenery, road conditions, and so on, are always the same. In road and criterium racing, there are too many variables to be looking backward over your shoulder. If you spend the last few seconds before a sprint looking backward toward competitors behind you, you could hit a pothole and crash. Also, unlike track sprinting, in road and criterium races you usually have more than one or two racers to keep an eye on.

The most effective method of keeping track of the few riders who are on your wheel is to look down between your legs, or under your arm and back toward them. This technique works best when you are down on the drops of the bars and leading the pack, or no more than a few riders from the lead. You can look back through your legs or under your arm for just a fraction of a second to see who is there and what they're doing. The beauty of this technique is that it doesn't interfere with basic riding style. You can repeatedly look back without taking attention off the road in front of you.

Looking between your legs allows you to watch a breakaway partner as you enter a sprint or go for a prime. It's pretty easy to keep track of the rider drafting. This can also be invaluable if you're leading out a teammate for a prime or final sprint. With all the fighting for position that goes on, a teammate who you're leading out might get bumped from your wheel. A quick check between your legs to see that those are his fork blades behind you can be your assurance. Of course, that doesn't always work. I was leading out a teammate for a prime at a race in Miami. At about 800 meters, I looked down and saw the two-tone forks of our team bikes and started my sprint. You can imagine how surprised and angry I was when someone else sprinted by me at 150 meters with *the same* two-tone forks! It helps to have some highly distinguishing feature on your fork blades to differentiate your team from the competition.

Looking under your arms allows you a quick glance at the position of more riders than the one out your wheel. A glance under the right arm and you should be able to see what's happening to the right and the rear of you. This technique is probably most helpful when looking back at chasers who are just a few seconds behind. It's tough to distinguish much from looking upside down under your arm, but it can make the difference when you're trying to hold off chasers for a prime or in the final moments of a race.

Turning your head to look back at a competitor can also be a tactical mistake. If you start to rotate your head to the left to look back at a rider, he could catch you off guard by attacking around your right side. I used this same technique after being frustrated by a racer who had a mirror attached to his glasses. He would keep track of the riders he was with as we went for prime sprints. After seeing how he moved his head to watch me for the sprint, I positioned myself for the sprints. The next several sprints he was moving his head all around trying to find me in his mirror. In the meantime, I was sprinting by him. If he had simply looked through his legs or under his arms, he could have monitored me the whole time.

Who's Side Are You on Anyway?

Sometimes we can be our own worst enemy. We get so caught up in the emotional aspect of a race that we don't think things through. This is why self-introspection is such a good habit after a race. You learn best from your mistakes.

It had been almost a year since I had been in a bicycle race. The previous four years were spent almost exclusively racing in professional or national-class events. This little race was the first local event I'd ridden in many years. I snuck into the Cat. II–III event with a Cat. IV license.

In the bigger pack, I figured I could blend into the crowd and no one would see me and see how I was doing (or how I was *not* doing, if you know what I mean). With less than a hundred miles a week of "training," I knew the race would be challenging enough.

Those guys could really go from the gun. I remembered what that was all about, only this time I was on the receiving end of the punishment. I settled into a comfortable position in the middle of the pack. Fifteen laps into the race the pace was still very fast. I looked around to see how I was doing. There wasn't anyone on my wheel. I was right at the back of the field. *Oops.*

Even though this was a Cat. II–III event, the race progressed in the same fashion I was accustomed to. By halfway, the pace had slowed considerably and I was now able to move up into the field. Soon, a breakaway or two went off the front. Now a small group stayed out for a couple of laps. It was time to get to the front.

When you sit back, analyze how a race is going, and disassociate yourself from the emotional aspect of the race, it's amazing how predictable it can be. It's the act of "reading a race."

The little breakaway got caught, and soon another small group moved off the front. I went to the front and attacked to catch them. A teammate of one of the riders ahead was chasing me down with the entire pack closely behind. Just before my pursuer caught me, I sat up and swung off in obvious defeat. He eased up and so did the rest of the pack behind. The next instant, I dropped it down two cogs and sprinted after the breakaway again. This time I was successful.

If there was a difference between the racing I was accustomed to and what was happening here, it was now apparent. The five of us were not working smoothly together. There was not the sense of urgency that accompanies a threatening breakaway in a professional race. Quickly establishing a lead discourages any prolonged chase effort from the pack. We were dangling off the front. My efforts to get the riders to work smoothly went right out the window when, of all things, a *pizza prime* was announced. These guys weren't really taking this seriously, were they? Apparently they were because the ensuing sprint *shattered* what was left of the breakaway. I guess not all racing is so calculable. Our pizza prime winner put his head down and tried to go for the solo win with fifteen laps remaining.

He clearly had the sprint. If this guy would've worked in the breakaway, he could have won the whole race. Now that he was off by himself, I figured I should teach him a lesson. I did all I could to keep him at that titillating distance— close enough so he wasn't a threat, but far enough ahead so he wouldn't give up.

We caught and dropped him with five to go. . . . Well, he *did* win a pizza that day.

CHAPTER 2
Pace Lines

If you learn just *one thing* from reading this book, this is it. Riding a pace line is fundamental to learning all of the other tricks of the trade. If you want to be a successful writer, at some point in your life you are going to have to learn the alphabet. This is similar. When it comes to successful bike racing, riding a pace line is—at the risk of sounding redundant—*fundamental*.

It's critical to know it inside and out and even to understand how to make a line work smoothly when someone in the line may not have the best rotating technique. The difference between a successful breakaway and getting caught is often how quickly you establish a smooth rolling pace line or echelon. As your breakaway is forming off the front of the pack, you're most vulnerable to being caught. Learn and practice all of these pace lines and echelons with your teammates or training partners. It's good practice and also good training.

The difference between a pace line and an echelon is that a pace line has each rider pull at the front of the line, anywhere from a few seconds to several minutes. In an echelon there's no pause at the front. The riders are continually moving in a circle. As soon as a rider hits the front of the line, he or she swings off and starts to move back in the line.

The basic pace line is the one you'll use most often. It's a straight rotation, most often used in a race or team time trial. Each rider takes a pull at the front and then swings off. While this seems simple enough, there are many details that can make the pace line considerably more efficient.

First, let's look at the dynamics of a pace line in a race situation (see Diagram 2.1). For all essential purposes, a team time trial and a breakaway are the same thing. Riders are working together at very close to their maximum capacity, either to put distance on a pack or to chase after a group in front. Either way the key is efficiency.

Diagram 2.1: Basic pace line

First, the pace line must remain at a steady speed. The line—that is, the riders lined up to draft—must maintain a constant pace. More specifically, it's not speed that's important but effort level. We'll talk in terms of speed because effort level is subjective. The point is, when the pace line is working smoothly at 29 mph on the flats and then you hit a grade, you can't have a guy at the front try to maintain the same speed; he'll blow or blow up the pace line.

Pulling Off

After his pull the rider at the front swings off. If there's any prevailing wind, the rider always pulls off into the wind (see Diagram 2.2). This is absolutely critical, because with any perceived crosswind, riders following are staggered downwind in the draft. To swing off other than into the wind means that the rider is crossing overlapped wheels. If there's no prevailing wind, the riders should pull off to a predetermined side. To change the side to which a rider pulls off without everyone knowing could be fatal. The unsuspecting rider pulling through may already be overlapping wheels, and a crash could result. The second rider in line is best able to feel any wind shift that would necessitate a change in the direction that the pace line pulls off. This second rider has to really shout out to make sure the rider in front and those who are following hear the command. If the rider in front decides it's necessary to pull off to a different side, the lead

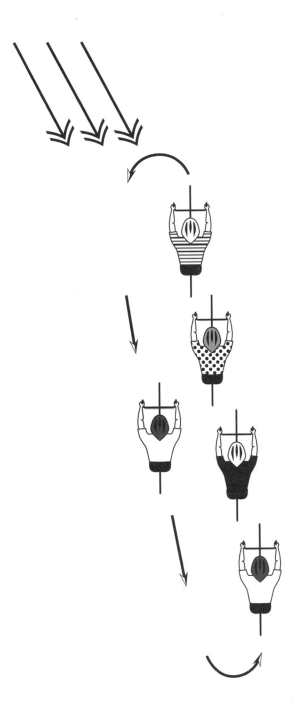

Diagram 2.2: The lead rider always pulls off into the wind.

rider should shout to the others the new direction. If there's no change in direction, nothing needs to be said.

When a rider pulls off the front, it must be in a steady and predictable fashion. You don't dive over or lurch off the front. The movement should be smooth; and yet it should still be completely apparent that you're pulling off and not just moving the pace line to a different position on the roadway.

When you pull off, you shouldn't swing way out into the road. You should simply pull over only far enough for the riders behind to move by you without having to steer around your handlebars.

There are two real reasons for keeping the pace line that close. First, it gives the rider moving through to take a pull of your draft a few more moments as he moves by you. You also benefit from catching a little of their draft as you move back to the end of the pace line. This small amount of added draft isn't insignificant. It adds up over the course of many miles of racing, especially when you're riding at close to your maximum effort level.

It's not always clear to following riders when you're pulling off the front. Shifting winds, winding roads, or approaching corners could contribute to a rider misjudging your movements. You don't want to have the second rider in line pulling through when you're still actively pulling at the front. It would be wasting the collective energy of the pace line to have two riders fighting the wind. And the second rider probably has to accelerate to start moving past you.

There are two almost universally recognized signals for pulling off at the front of a pace line. If the riders are in the draft directly behind one another, the lead rider can flick his elbow out to the side indicating he's about to swing off. You should always use your elbow to signal the direction you're pulling off to. This is because if there were any slight crosswind, the riders following, staggered downwind, would easily see the signal. In those situations where the trailing riders are staggered slightly, you need to only signal by flipping your fingers out. They can easily see your hands on the handlebars.

Pull Duration

There is no absolute standard for the length of a pull. You must factor many things when you consider how long you want to pull. You can pull as long as you want, but if you start to tire and your pace starts to drop, as little as 0.5 mph, you should swing off and let the next person pull through. In team time trial training, we have found that thirty pedal strokes is about optimum. This equates to about 25 seconds on the front.

You must consider wind. A stronger headwind and you're going to want to pull less. Conversely, a tailwind means you might want to pull longer. After all, 100-kilometer team time trials are often won by scant seconds and each time a rider pulls off the front, the team is essentially forfeiting one bike length. (Think about that for a minute if you don't understand the significance.) You have to find a happy medium between these factors.

Getting Back On

Once you are off the front, soft-pedal until you reach the back of the line, where you should reaccelerate and move into the draft of the last rider. Here again, it sounds like pretty simple stuff, but there are various factors to keep in mind. First, there's the speed at which you're decelerating. In a pace line each rider can determine this for himself. It should be at a pace that's physically less demanding, but not so slow that when it's time to get back on the pace line the acceleration is a big effort. You'll have to experiment. Soft-pedaling—spinning the pedals but not actually applying pressure—works best in most cases.

Fine-Tuning

Pace lines can work well in training, going along at 60 percent effort. Efficiency is another matter when you start to go harder. Any little mistake you or your fellow pace line partners make is amplified. Suddenly, what once looked like a well-oiled machine falls into chaos. This is where work on the finer details makes all the difference. Here are some of the most common mistakes.

Even the most seasoned cyclist can mistakenly pull off to the wrong side. If the movement is smooth and predictable and the riders following are not dangerously overlapping his rear wheel, the best way to quickly recover is for the following riders to go ahead and pull through. It's more confusing and dangerous to have the rider who just pulled off swing back across the pace line. If you make a mistake and pull off to the wrong side, don't try to correct it. Just signal the next rider through.

Duration and speed of the pull at the front take a great deal of practice and practical experience to master. The effort level must remain fairly constant. The most common mistake is for the rider sitting in second spot to get excited and want to accelerate through as soon as the lead rider swings off. Don't accelerate the pace; then every other rider will have to accelerate. We've probably all been in pace lines that yo-yo back and forth, so we're constantly accelerating or hitting the brakes to stay on the rider in front. This is caused by riders accelerating as they pull through and then tiring and slowing down at the end of their pull. If a rider in the pace line is tired or weak, he should pull shorter. If a rider is feeling strong and fresh he should pull longer but not necessarily faster.

All the members of my winning team at the national team time trial championships in 1981 were very balanced, but one of the riders was having a bad day. After 50 kilometers, this rider's pulls had to be cut to only 10 seconds. Ron Kiefel was feeling the strongest and his pulls were averaging longer than anyone else's, about 30 seconds to my 20 seconds. The point was, we were keeping the pace and the speed very steady with the weaker rider taking a very short pull and the stronger rider taking a longer pull.

There's always the tendency for the stronger rider to want to pick up the speed. In some cases that might be necessary, so try and keep the pace line together and accelerate very gradually. Imagine (maybe you don't have to imagine because you've experienced it personally) what it would feel like to be one of the weaker riders in a pace line, to have just pulled your hardest, swung off, and as you're working to get to the back of the line the guy in front is punching the accelerator.

Another common mistake occurs when the rider drifting back after a pull has to accelerate to get back on. Don't wait until your front wheel is even with the last rider's rear wheel to start accelerating. When to start your acceleration depends on your speed in relation to the rider you have to slip in behind. A good guideline is to start the acceleration as your front wheel comes even with the last rider's bottom bracket. You learn to adjust this as you become more sensitive to the flow of the pace line.

Before we won the national team time trial championships, the four of us rode for over a month together, always following the same rotation we would use in our race. We were so skilled at pace line rotation that when I accelerated onto the back of Ron Kiefel's wheel, our tires would occasionally brush sidewalls. In a standard race situation you can't afford to ride *that* closely to another rider because he might make a sudden move to the side. But this does give you an idea how closely you would like to follow if possible.

After a pull, most riders drop back too far to the side. Stay close, both from side to side and also in the draft.

Double Pace Line

A double pace line is the line we most often use for training. Riders are two abreast, and the other riders are in file behind them (see Diagram 2.3). This double pace line is really used for social reasons. You can ride miles and miles and have someone to talk with as you do. All of the characteristics of the single pace line are the same as the double except that when the riders pull off the front the riders always swing off to their respective sides. The cyclist leading on the right pace line always pulls off to the right; the one on the left always pulls off to the left. In training rides with this double pace line, it's obvious which riders follow too far behind. When someone can't sit closely behind a wheel (most likely a result of fear or poor bike handling skills) the pace line has a hard time staying two abreast.

Because the double pace line is used for training purposes, the duration of time two riders sit on the front is subject to the objectives of the group training. The pulls can be 30 seconds or 30 minutes.

Pace Line Tactics

Believe it or not, there are some tactics that you can employ while riding in a pace line. We've discussed how to run a

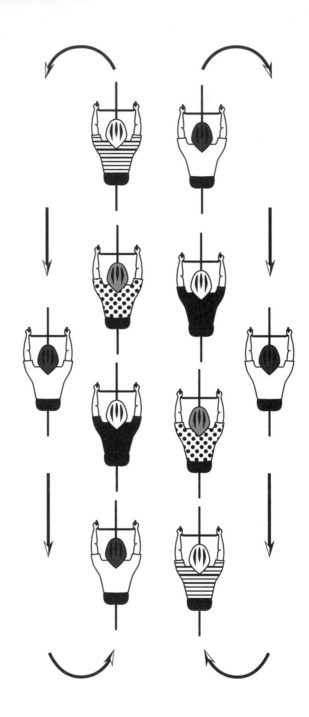

Diagram 2.3: Double pace line

smooth pace line, and in most cases that's all you'll want to do. But what if you are in a breakaway with three or four other racers from different teams? In Chapter 3 I will cover how you can work with other riders to form successful breakaways and how you can use their strengths to your advantage. How do you slow the pace line down? What if you want to wear out the other riders to set yourself up for an attack? There are pace line tactics for each of these scenarios.

Slowing down a pace line is relatively easy (also see Chapter 4 on blocking). You simply need to cause interruptions. You can allow gaps to open, you can pull through too slowly, and so on. Now let's say you are in a pace line and there is one rider who is really strong and making you hurt with his pulls. Your best tactic is to reposition yourself where that rider will cause you less damage. The worst position in the pace line would be directly in front or directly behind the strong racer (see Diagram 2.4). If you are pulling off just before the strong racer hits the front you're likely to be fighting harder to get back onto the pace line. When you pull through following the strongest rider in the pace line, you will probably hit the front and the wind at an uncomfortable speed. Try to position yourself so that other riders are both before and after the stronger rider.

Again, speed is often irrelevant in pace lines. Effort level is what counts. When a pace line is moving along smoothly, riders are most likely at different levels of their maximum effort.

Diagram 2.4: Rider A is the strongest in the pace line. The riders in the dark jerseys will have to work harder than the rider in the polka-dot jersey.

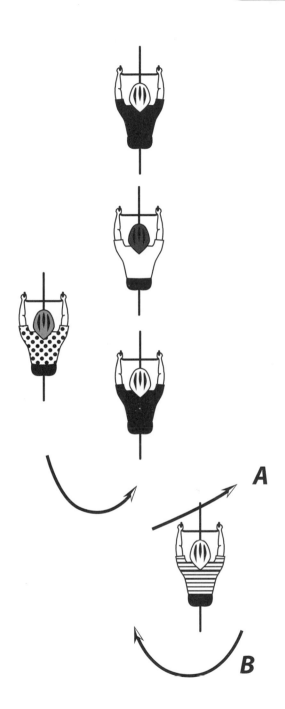

Diagram 2.5: To rest a little in a pace line, the rider at the rear would pull off the back just a bit (see arrow A) and signal the rider dropping back to take his place before slipping back into position B.

Many riders make the mistake of not gauging their speed as they approach a hill. I often see riders remain in a pace line as it starts up a hill in spite of the fact that they are approaching their max. The effort level that was comfortable on the flat roadway is now too great. Rather than sit out a pull or two, they continue until they reach the front of the pace line, hit the wind, blow up, and then they never get back on the end of the line. Anticipate the effort that is going to be required. If you are feeling tired, if you need a little rest to grab a bite to eat, wave a few riders into the line ahead of you (see Diagram 2.5).

Echelons

Echelons are the most complex form of a pace line. Whereas each rider in a regular pace line takes a pull of any length and then swings off, in the echelon the rider at the front doesn't pause there. As soon as a rider is on the front, he's pulling off. This puts all of the riders in continuous motion in relationship to one another. The formation looks like a circle (see Diagram 2.6), with riders moving either clockwise or counterclockwise depending on any wind. There's one line moving forward, which we will call the fast lane, and another line of riders moving backward, which we'll refer to as the slow lane. A rider is in constant motion. Echelons are the most difficult to master and the most fun to ride in.

Echelons require a lot of practice and concentration to perform. Certain European races are noted for windy road

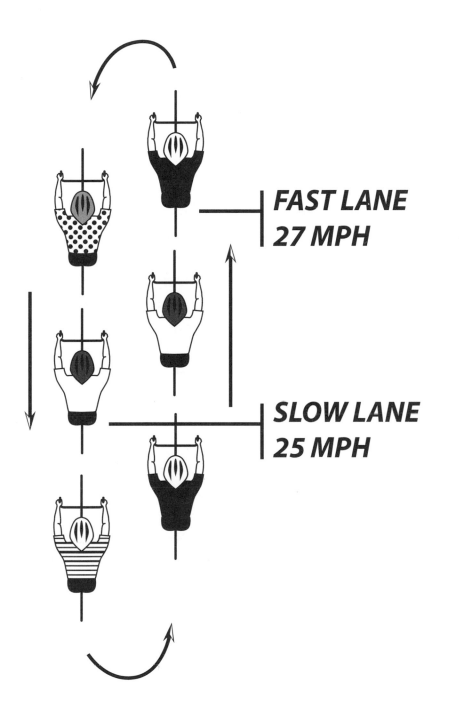

**FAST LANE
27 MPH**

**SLOW LANE
25 MPH**

Diagram 2.6: Basic echelon formation

races that splinter the pack of international racers into small groups. It's in windy, especially crosswind, situations that echelon riding is all-important.

I can recall a time we were racing across the barren, wind-swept country on narrow single-lane roads. The winds had split the field into several small echelons that were working closely together. I thought I was doing fine, holding my own against Europeans who were vastly more experienced at that point in my career. I knew how to ride in a crosswind, but in these echelons a rider had to constantly fight for position or get forced off the back and out of the draft. My technique wasn't very polished, and it irritated the English racer sitting on my wheel. He yelled something to me, and I turned around to ask what the problem was. That tiny lapse in con-centration was all it took. The next thing I knew, the English rider and I were several meters off the back of the group, fighting the wind on our own. It took us about 1 mile to work our way back into the echelon.

The stronger the crosswind, the more critical it is to get into a smooth working echelon. This played out at a stage in a race held in Texas several years ago. The point-to-point road race traveled 80 miles heading due east. The fact that the wind was blowing about 10 mph from the north didn't go unnoticed by the elite racers in the field. At the starter's pistol there was a flurry of activity at the front of the 100-man field. Less than 2 miles into the race, about two dozen racers formed a tight echelon and started pulling away from the rest of the pack. With each mile we opened up an increasing gap on the chasers. In less than 5 miles the outcome was obvious. The race was over for all of the cyclists behind the lead echelon. A group of riders working together smoothly are no match for a string of riders fighting the wind individually.

HOW ECHELONS WORK

First, let's look at the straight echelon. It's very similar to the regular pace line described earlier in this chapter. Riders are positioned one behind the other. But in an echelon, as soon as a rider reaches the front of the line and hits the wind, he pulls off to the side and starts a slow drift to the back of the line. In a pace line the rider at the front can pull into the wind as long as he likes, whether a few seconds or several minutes. No one ever sits on the front of an echelon; the lead constantly changes. Chapter 5 goes into greater detail on this subject.

The second factor that distinguishes a pace line from an echelon is how the riders drop back once they have pulled through. In the pace line a rider can drop back at his own pace, reaching the back of the line as hastily or leisurely as he chooses. In the echelon all aspects of the formation must be coordinated with the other riders. As soon as one rider has pulled off the front and starts to drop back, another rider pulls off. Rotating in this fashion places each rider in the wind for only a few seconds. As the rider drops back in the line, they're protected from the wind by sitting in the draft of the rider in front of them, who is also dropping back.

While this may sound easy, there are many different levels of mastery to ride in an echelon. You can go out on an easy training ride and feel completely proficient with your teammates, but when you find yourself in a breakaway during a race, rotating in an echelon can become entirely foreign. At training speed you can physically compensate for any slight mistakes you make. When you're in a race, the echelon is moving at maximum speed and most of the riders are just about at their physical max. If you're not getting the most out of the draft as you drop back, or if you don't get on the back of the line at just the right time, you will waste a lot of energy. Just as the English racer and I found ourselves off the back from my moment's lapse in concentration, little mistakes in an echelon are amplified because the riders must work together so closely.

Because echelons are so difficult to master and necessitate riding so tightly, I advise practicing whenever you get the opportunity. First, you should become proficient at a straight echelon without any wind.

PULLING THROUGH AND OFF

The pull through and off the front is one of the most crucial maneuvers of the echelon. Timing and pace are everything.

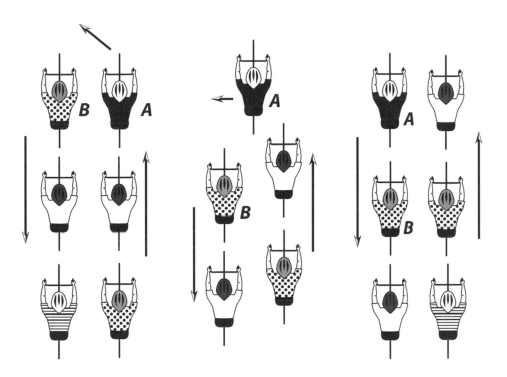

Diagram 2.7: Rider A is going slightly faster than rider B. The perception is that rider A is pulling off in front of rider B. As rider A moves off the front of the fast lane, he or she moves left and slows slightly. Once in the slow lane, rider A will maintain the same speed until the next rider moves off the front.

First, the pull at the front is going to be very short. You may be tempted to accelerate as the rider in front of you pulls off. Don't! The pace in each line of the echelon—the line moving forward and the line moving backward—must stay constant. For example, the line moving *into the wind* forward might stay constant about 27 mph. The line dropping back would hover about 25 mph. (It's very helpful to have a cycle computer on your bike to monitor your speed as you pull through. Of course it is most important to stay on the wheel and in the draft of the rider directly in front of you.) Pulling off at just the right moment takes coordinated effort and timing for both rider A and rider B (see Diagram 2.7). Executed perfectly, rider A pulls off and eases right in front of rider B as he passes backward. The rear wheel of rider A pulling off, moves directly in front of the front wheel of rider B, who is dropping back. As rider A moves out of the faster "pulling" lane and into the slower "drop back" lane, he must change his speed to that of the slower moving lane.

These two riders share the responsibility of a smooth change. First, rider A must time his pull off the front to avoid swinging over too soon and chopping the wheel of rider B, or pulling too long and making rider B hang out in the wind. Rider B must not drop back too far or too quickly, as it would cause a gap between him and rider A as they drop back in the slower lane.

The exact time rider A swings over depends on how fast the echelon is moving and rotating. It takes practice to get a feel for just the right time; but if you wait until your wheel is completely in front of the other rider's front wheel before you swing off, it will be too late. A general guideline would be for rider A to start moving over as the axle of his rear wheel moves parallel with the front axle of rider B.

GETTING BACK ON

As each rider drops back he should be completely protected from the wind, in a draft, by following a wheel in front of him. The next critical point is the move back into the echelon's fast lane. Again, this takes concentration because if you're not paying attention, the last rider in the fast lane could pass by you and you would then have to close a gap to get back into the draft. Once an echelon is established you can simply remember the order of the rotation and know when the last rider in the echelon, the rider who is directly behind you in the slow lane, is approaching. Until that order has been established you must keep tabs on the faster-moving lane as you're dropping back.

Just as you anticipate swinging off the front of the lane, you should also anticipate getting back into the fast lane (see Diagram 2.8). If you wait to accelerate until the last rider in the fast lane has completely moved past you, you have waited

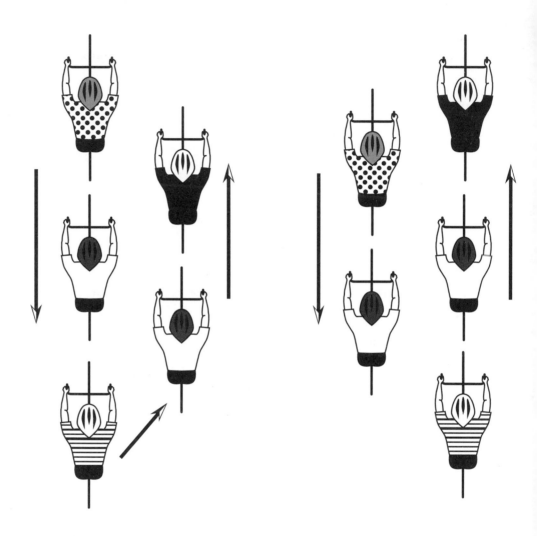

Diagram 2.8: Moving back into the fast lane of an echelon

too long. As a general guideline, start accelerating to the speed of the faster lane when your front axle is parallel with the last rider's bottom bracket. As you start increasing your speed, you'll ease over into the other lane, and hopefully directly into the draft. Experiment with the exact timing of this to find what is right for you and the echelon situation you're in.

CROSSWIND ECHELON

When the wind is blowing from the side, the echelon must change to a crosswind position, which is the most difficult type. The standard echelon has the riders moving in a constant rotation. The crosswind echelon is the same, but now to stay in the draft each rider is staggered off to the side. The riders are moving forward and backward, but also diagonally across the road (see Diagram 2.9). The whole procedure of moving in the echelon front to back in a lane and diagonally across the road is simplified by following the wheel in front of you and staying in the proper draft.

As with any pace line or echelon, the lead rider always pulls off *into* any prevailing wind. To do anything else would mean crossing over a wheel and possibly causing a crash. The major difference in a crosswind echelon is how the riders are staggered across the roadway and the degree to which they are staggered is based solely on wind direction. A slight wind from the left means the riders will need to be slightly staggered off

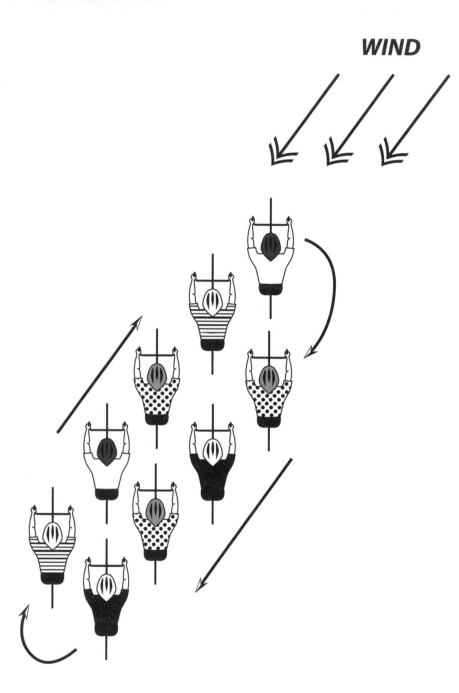

WIND

Diagram 2.9: Crosswind echelon

to the right. A strong wind from the left flank makes the proper draft farther to the side of a rider, and the echelon will be staggered more pronouncedly to the right.

Swinging off, dropping back, and then getting back on are similar to a standard echelon with a few modifications. When a rider swings off the front, he doesn't need to pull off very far. The riders are already staggered, so moving over slightly gives the next rider enough room to pull through. To get back on the back of a crosswind echelon takes more skill and energy because of the way the echelon rotates. To get back on you will be restrained from accelerating and getting into the draft until the last rider's rear wheel has moved completely past your front wheel (see Diagram 2.10).

This very critical transition in the echelon is where I made my mistake in the European race, by not paying attention as I was about to jump back on. When you're in a crosswind echelon, getting on at the back can actually be more difficult than pulling through at the front. At the front you are in someone's draft for all but a few seconds, then you're pulling off and starting to slow down.

You can make the transition to the back of the echelon easier by preparing yourself as rider B is approaching. Get out of the saddle as if you are about to do a jump or an acceleration. Just before rider B's wheel passes, start to accelerate. When you have just enough room, slide over into the proper place and sit down, throwing the bike forward into

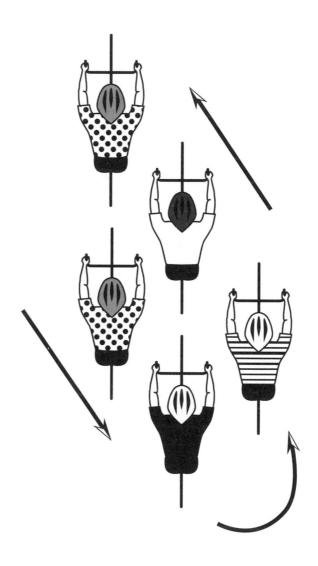

Diagram 2.10: Pulling off and getting back on in a crosswind
echelon

the draft. You can even increase the efficiency of this transition by riding closer to rider B's rear wheel, throwing the bike backward as your front wheel crosses behind, and then sitting down and throwing the bike forward into his draft. (See section drills in Chapter 12 for more detail.)

CHANGES IN WIND DIRECTION

In a crosswind echelon it is rare for the wind not to shift and cause you to adjust your position relative to the rider in front of you. Whether it's an actual wind shift or a bend in the road, the configuration of the echelon will change accordingly. The important thing is for you to stay in the proper draft (as if you don't already have enough to think about!). In a crosswind echelon, keep moving around slightly until you find the exact draft (see Diagram 2.11).

Major wind shifts require the echelon to alter its rotation. For example, if the wind is coming from the right, the echelon will be staggered off to the left (see Diagram 2.12). When riders come to a bend in the road, the wind is now hitting them on their left side. The first rider to feel the wind shift pulls off in the opposite direction. The last rider who pulled off to the previous direction must fall back and get into the rotation without the assistance of any draft. The echelon follows its normal rotation to the new side. This rotation continues until the wind direction dictates another change.

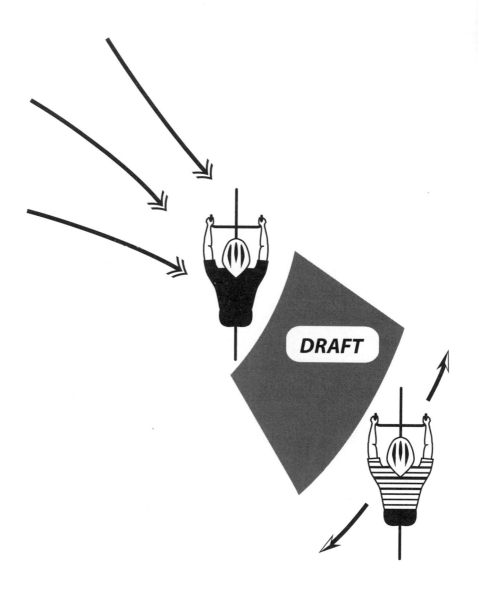

Diagram 2.11: Finding the proper draft in a crosswind echelon

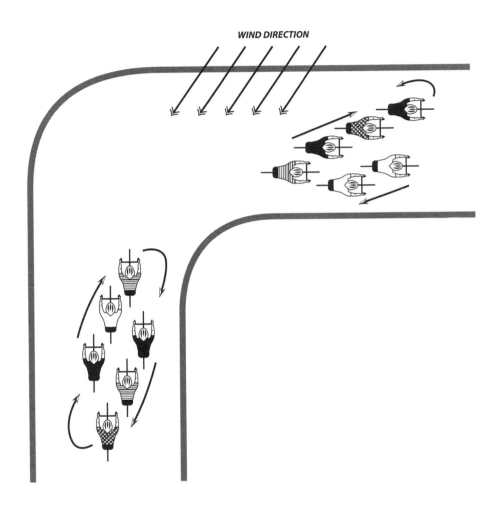

WIND DIRECTION

Diagram 2.12: Effects of a major wind shift on the configuration
of an echelon

Common Problems in Echelons

There are many details to learn about riding in an echelon. It's imperative to concentrate on all of the aspects of the echelon. Because of the complexity involved, you should work with teammates and training partners to fine-tune technique. As you pull through, have the rider behind you give you a quick critique.

In summary, here are the common problems to avoid:

- Don't jump through at the front. Keep the pace or effort constant as you pull through.
- Don't start slowing down before you pull off the front. It will cause the riders behind you to slow down and then accelerate.
- Don't swing off too far. Keep the echelon tight. You can also get a draft from riders beside you.
- Don't drop back too fast.
- Don't drift off the wheel in front of you as you drop back.
- Start your acceleration before you get back onto the back of the echelon.
- Make sure you're really in the optimum draft. Move around (gingerly) to be sure.
- Never make sudden moves.

Echelons are difficult to master. They take individual expertise and also a high level of group talent. Critical maneuvers aren't taking place every 20 or 30 seconds, as with a pace line, but continuously and by every rider. Throw in some rolling hills or a few corners and you begin to understand how challenging racing in a smooth echelon can be—not just physically, but mentally. It takes practice.

CHAPTER 3
Breaking Away

Getting the Jump

It wasn't until I was in a race in Europe that this very simple, very basic, maneuver occurred to me.

I was in a road race and having a tough time of it. The pace was fast, but what was bothering me was the constant attacks being launched from the field. It seemed like I was always closing a gap on the rider in front of me. One rider in particular, a Swede, had incredible speed. If I wasn't *right* on his wheel when he jumped, it was all over. I could never catch him. Then we were all strung out in single file, with the Swede at the front, when he jumped hard. What I observed next changed the way I would try to respond to attacks and negotiate corners from then on.

Have you ever been sitting in your car at a red light, behind seven other cars waiting for the light to turn green? When it does and the first car moves through the intersection and the second car starts to roll forward, there is a moment's delay. Then the third car starts to move. By the time you can start to move, the light has already turned yellow and you won't get through the intersection until the next green light.

Now, imagine how many more cars would make it through the intersection if everyone applied pressure to the gas pedal at the same time. You could blame your being late to work on the slow reaction times of the other drivers in front of you and their cars overcoming inertia. It's the same thing in bike racing. When someone jumps at the front of a line of riders, the following rider has to react, which takes a moment. Then he has to respond and accelerate himself and the bike, which takes both time and effort. This delayed effect continues down the line of racers. If you're somewhere down the line, by the time you start to jump there's a slight gap between each rider and, most importantly, a gap ahead of you. As you're trying to close the gap, the racers ahead are also trying to close the gaps in front of them (see Diagram 3.1, B). This is both tiring and a total waste of energy.

When you multiply this extra effort for each attack, by the time the end of the race comes you're going to be more tired. To respond to each attack from the front of the pack always requires effort and energy to match the move. There's a way to narrow the gap between you and the racer directly in front of you, and it actually saves energy expenditure.

If you moved simultaneously with the rider directly in front of you, accelerating at the same instant he or she did, matching the move with the same speed as the racer in front of you, you wouldn't lose any ground (see Diagram 3.1, C & D). You wouldn't find yourself having to jump and close a gap at the same time. This is significant, because you won't be out of a draft, saving about 20 to 30 percent of energy expended while closing a gap. Think about that: 20 to 30 percent. That is a lot and it can add up.

Timing, Timing, Timing

It's all in the timing. It'll take some practice to see just when you need to start your jump in order to not lose the wheel of the rider in front. You might want to practice this a little when you're out riding with a group of teammates doing jumps or sprints. But the only time and place you can really hone this technique is during a race. Race situations are

A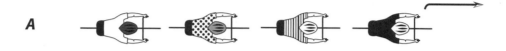

B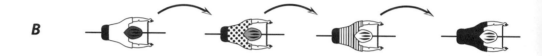

C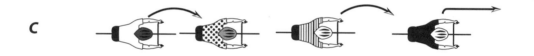

D

Diagram 3.1

A: The rider in the front attacks.

B: Each rider jumps following the racer in front of him.

C: The fourth rider anticipates the jump and starts accelerating early.

D: The fourth rider stays in the draft of the rider in front of him as the acceleration in the line takes place, thereby saving energy.

always different and your competitors respond differently to attacks than do your teammates and riding buddies.

To start with, try initiating your jump when the rider *two* places in front of you starts to move. If the rider directly in front of you responds in a typical fashion, you might just have the timing correct so as he starts to accelerate, you move with him in his draft. Try making your effort at varying moments until you seem to hit on the right moment to start the jump. Obviously, we're talking about fractions of seconds.

Timing a Corner

Your jump doesn't have to be in response to any special attack. This whole delayed response action I'm talking about happens on corners as well. In a corner, it's actually much more pronounced, because as a pack of racers approaches a corner, they slow down. The farther back you are in the pack, the more you have to slow down. As the racers jump out of the corner in front of you, it's as if they were responding to someone attacking. You can anticipate this jump by a fraction of a second and stay safely tucked in the draft. Try and hone this technique on every corner of a criterium. It'll make the race an easier effort in the long run.

So what if the guy in front doesn't respond at all? Or what if the guy in front is doing the same thing you are? This is where practice and fast reactions will pay off. If you're jumping at the same instant as the rider in front of you, you're narrowing your room for error. You must be ready to respond to the jump, the same way you have to respond instantaneously when you're sitting inches from someone's rear wheel. This again takes a little practice and solid concentration.

When you initiate your jump, anticipating the rider in front of you, and he doesn't respond, you should move off to the right or left side, getting by him with as little loss of speed as possible. Your premature jump will be that much more helpful starting you on your way to closing the even larger gap in front of you. Besides, if the rider in front of you doesn't respond to a jump, more than likely you'll want to be in front of him anyway.

If the racer just ahead is experienced in this technique and anticipates the racer in front of him, you must be that much quicker and that much more aware of what's going on directly ahead of you. In a racing situation, you need to find the correct timing of your reaction. When some racer in front of you breaks that rhythm, either by not reacting or by moving more quickly than you're used to, make a mental note of their race number so you'll be ready the next time you find yourself behind them.

The Keys to Success

Successful breakaways are almost always the result of a combination of physical strength and tactical timing . . . *and*, maybe, a little bit of luck.

You must establish your own definition of a successful breakaway. It could be your intention to only stay off the front of a chasing pack for a few miles to nab a prime sprint, or it could be to make the move to win the race from 30 miles out. For our discussion, we simply have to consider that the breakaway rider or riders are moving away from the chasers and building a lead. There are numerous factors that determine the who, how, and when of a breakaway. Since you probably notice that it's often the same racers consistently getting in breakaways, let's consider *luck* to be the least significant factor in determining a break's success.

Attacks and subsequent successful breakaways are a lot like shots at a goal, or a basketball tossed at a hoop—the more often you try, the higher the chances of success. The racers that are most often found in successful breakaways are usually the ones that are in the unsuccessful attacks, as well. Think of "poor" Jacky Durand if you want inspiration. Sure, he's known as the "King of the Head Bangers"—those guys that constantly try seemingly futile attacks—but *every once in a while*, Jacky made one stick and he scored wins that men of the same talent and fitness would never dream of earning.

When the determining factor in the success of a breakaway is a racer's strength or specific ability, there isn't much we can discuss. Breakaways like climbing over a mountain pass or solo moves don't develop from much tactical maneuvering. Either you have to stay off the front alone or with the leaders on the hill, or you don't. There are ways you can increase your chances in both instances, but that's another story.

Quite often, what distinguishes one winning breakaway from just another unsuccessful attack is a few simple techniques and a little extra effort.

Allies or Rivals?

The first thing to look for when a breakaway is starting to form is the combination of riders in the lead. Before you expend a lot of your own energy, you need to evaluate the situation. Are these racers going to be willing to work together? A four-man group might *look* good with two riders from Team "A," another from Team "B," and you from another team. But what happens if a strong rivalry exists between Teams A and B? The Team B rider probably won't work in a situation where he is outnumbered by rivals. While *you* might feel comfortable working in this break, the Team A riders, even with a numerical advantage, might just sit up and get caught before they give anyone from Team B a free ride to the finish line.

Allies Behind?

Another question to ask yourself is: Do any of the riders in the break have teammates back in the pack that will likely block and increase your chances of success? Ideally, you want to get away with a rider or two from a strong team that works well together.

Let's look at specific situations from races that might have happened this year in the United States. You're in a three-man break in a criterium with one, say, Colavita-Bolla racer and another from Sierra Nevada. The riders you're with have the strength to make the break work, you're all willing to work together, and between the three teams, there are plenty of riders to block. Unfortunately, without a Health Net rider represented in that break, the escaping trio is still very likely to be chased down.

Still, this is a breakaway situation that you want to work with. Indeed, Health Net might launch a racer up to the three of you without dragging along the pack, and then your odds of success would be tremendous . . . and that is precisely what you're doing, playing the odds.

Each attack you make is a gamble, increasing your odds of success. Each break that has the right combination of racers also increases those odds.

Years ago in my own racing career, during the Key Biscayne Triumph Road Race—a very flat and fast race—a group of a dozen riders split off the front of the pack less than 10 miles into a 75-mile event. From the start, there were countless attacks from the talented field, one right after the other. With the speed averaging over 30 miles per hour, it seemed unlikely that anything could stay off the front, especially so early in the race with so much strength in the pack. But when the dozen opened up a small gap, the peloton uncharacteristically eased up for a few miles. A quick look at the jerseys in the breakaway told why. There was exactly one rider from each of the strong teams. No one was chasing because those teams already had one rider represented; no one was blocking because with only one rider in the break out of twelve, the odds didn't dictate that a teammate behind the breakaway should expend energy for his teammate. That breakaway ended up finishing about 10 minutes clear of the next group of fifteen, which also had about the same spread of riders from all the teams.

Staying Power?

Whenever you find yourself in a break, you will need to ask yourself whether your companions are strong enough or fast enough to make it to the end. Even if they aren't, it doesn't mean you shouldn't work with them. If some other rider is willing to work and you can use that to your advantage, by all means, do it!

I once got into an early breakaway with three other racers during a stage race in Australia. We continually opened up a gap on the pack but it was obvious that my break companions weren't going to sustain the pace or stay away to the finish line. After 20 miles, and with 30 more to go, it was down to just one fading Australian and me. I tempered my effort so as not to do too much more work than the other racer. I also kept close tabs on the time splits of the pack. When our time started to decrease, and it was obvious that the other racer was completely spent and had nothing more to offer, I attacked with a six-and-a-half-minute lead on the pack. I held off the pack to the finish line and won by about a minute and a half.

Time to Work Together

If a breakaway is going to work, it's absolutely essential that the riders who are off the front of the pack start working together immediately. For an example, we'll use the case of four racers, each from different teams, who after a series of attacks establish a small gap over the rest of the field. The four must start working like a team time trial team—everyone sharing the pace and the workload. In the rotation of the four racers, if one guy decides not to pull through and opens up a gap in the pace line, it would create a stall in their speed. Depending on the margin, that momentary stall could be enough to drop the break back within the reach of the pack.

If you are in that breakaway situation, a little extra effort on your part could make the difference for success. If you're coming back in the pace line and you see that one of the guys is sitting up, slip into the spot (see Diagram 3.2) and take an extra pull. Your breakaway companion who didn't take a turn might need just a momentary rest. Or, let's say that everyone has just pulled and are sitting behind the lead rider. The lead rider is finishing his pull and is slowing down to drop back into the last spot, and everyone is slowing with him. If you

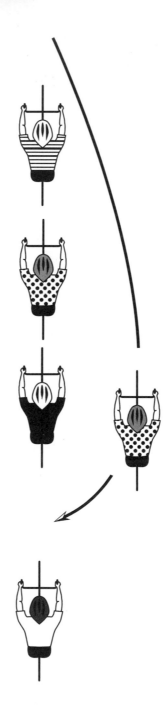

Diagram 3.2: Slipping into a gap in a pace line

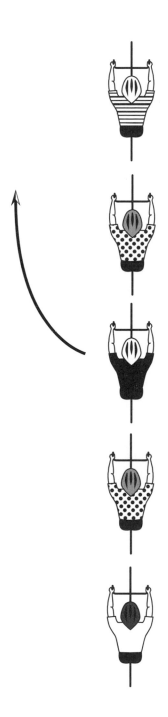

Diagram 3.3: Restarting the pace line rotation

don't see the gap open up, or you're already in line and it looks like no one is going to take the initiative to start the pace line again, ease out of the line and move to the front with the riders behind you still on your wheel. Start the pace line rotation again (see Diagram 3.3). If the racer(s) continues to sit on and not share the work, it's time to reevaluate the breakaway situation.

Pulling through smoothly in a breakaway is also critical. Erratic speeds can drain both you and your fellow breakaway companions. Changes in speed can cause a racer who's close to his anaerobic threshold to go into oxygen debt, requiring some recovery and further slowing the break. If someone feels better in the break, they should pull longer at the same speed, or slowly pick up the pace over the course of the pull.

The important thing is to prevent someone *jumping* through on their pull. Conversely, if someone is not feeling as strong or fast, their pull should be shorter but not any slower. Even a short pull will give the others in the break a needed rest.

Corners Are an Asset

Corners are an opportunity for a breakaway group to open up more time on the pack. A small group can negotiate a corner faster than the whole pack, so it's important to take the advantage. Timing is important here, too. In most situations, don't

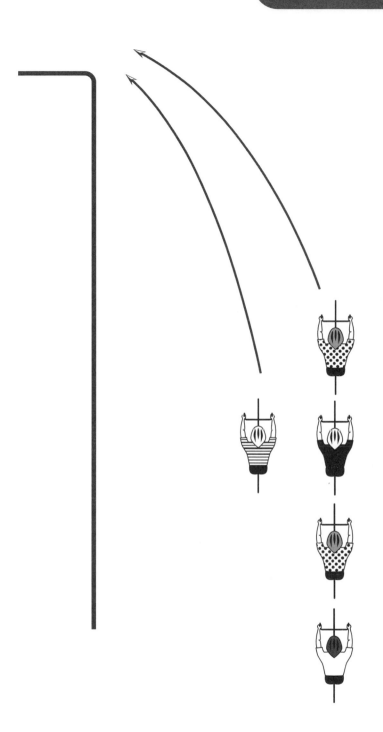

Diagram 3.4: Taking advantage of a corner with a breakaway group

pull off just before a corner. Pulling through the corner at the fastest safe speed will give the breakaway the most advantage. If you do have to pull off before the corner, pull to the outside of the corner (see Diagram 3.4). If you pull off to the inside of the corner, you'll block the rest of the group trying to speed through the corner.

Tactics within the Group

We've already discussed how to run a smooth pace line. In almost all cases, that's all you'll want to do, keeping in mind you are working with other riders to form successful breakaways and how you can use their strengths to your advantage. But what if you don't want the break to succeed? What do you do in a breakaway with three or four other racers from different teams? What about when you want to, or need to, slow the pace line down? What if you want to tire out the other riders to set yourself up for an attack? There are ways to accomplish these goals.

To slow down a pace line is pretty easy (see Chapter 4 on blocking). You simply need to get in the way of its functioning smoothly. You can let gaps open up, or you can pull through a little too slowly.

Now let's say you're in a pace line with one rider who is really strong and making you hurt with his pulls. Your best tactic is to position yourself where that rider will hurt you least. The worst positions to place yourself in the pace line would be directly in front of or directly behind the strong racer.

Again, it's important to find the right spot in the group. Pulling off as the strongest rider starts his pull will mean that you will be fighting to get back on the pace line. When you pull through following the strongest rider in the pace line, you're likely to hit the front and the wind at an uncomfortably fast speed. Find a position behind a weaker rider. Hopefully that will also leave at least one rider to pull through after you, before the strong rider hits the front.

Speed is really irrelevant in a pace line—it's the *effort* that counts. Given the disparity in talent, fitness, and levels of fatigue, it's likely that a smooth pace line requires participants to expend different levels of effort. Don't stare at your speedometer to determine your work load—try to gauge how you feel. As I've said before: This is especially critical as a group of riders approaches a hill.

What was manageable in the flats can throw you over the edge as the terrain steepens. Sit out one pull or even two, otherwise you run the risk of blowing up and then getting blown off the back.

Try to anticipate the level of work required. If you're tired, if you need a little rest or to grab a bite to eat, ease off and let a couple of riders past. You're not there to make friends. It's better to annoy the others than it is to get dropped.

Unwelcome Guests

So you're in a break with someone who is doing little or nothing to aid your effort. It may come down to the point where you need to lose this guy and that can be real frustrating.

Most likely, this situation develops out of a two-man breakaway. You're going to have to find that initial 5 or 10 seconds on your opponent. Let's review the probable situation from that breakaway.

First of all, you're probably already getting close to an all-out effort, if you're concerned about staying away. So how do you get rid of someone who's just hanging on with you? Before you start trying to ditch him, you need to mentally review the situation. Do you really want to drop him? If he's working at about an equal level with you, it might not be a very good idea. Even if he isn't, you have to ask yourself if he has teammates in the pack that might be blocking for the two of you.

For matters of this discussion, our goal here is to force the other rider into a situation where he has to chase after you, so you're both expending an equal amount of energy.

Before you make this effort, however, you may need to consider the consequences. First off, are you stronger than your opponent? This is especially important to consider when he's been sitting on your wheel and not doing any work. If he's stronger, you should assess the situation again. What are you doing all the work for? (Shame on you! We'll discuss this another time.)

Of course, you also have to consider the consequences of success. If you do dump this rider, will you lose help back in the field? Is his team blocking now? If so, you're bound to lose that if you scamper off on your own.

Once you have really determined that you want to get rid of him, you now have to assess him as a competitor. What are his strengths and weaknesses? If you don't know, it's even more important to know *your own* strengths and weaknesses. Now, how long is it to the finish or prime sprint you're targeting for? Can you hold on alone until then? Finally, do you make one big attack or do you make several attacks to wear him out?

For the sake of discussion, you've now established a little lead over your opponent. The two of you are each in what amounts to a time trial situation. Now is when you might be able to play some psychological games with him. At this point your goal is to demoralize.

A little-known truth about bicycle racing psychology: Your opponent is probably hurting just as much as you are . . . and maybe a little worse.

After holding your little gap steady for a few minutes, make an *acceleration*. Sure, you're hurting, but remember, so is he. A subtle acceleration will probably cause him to think that he's slowing down. If you can hold it just long enough, he might crack and give up the chase. That's what you're looking for, because you're going to have to ease off for a few moments to recover from the effort. This tactic is not one designed for energy efficiency. In fact, it's less efficient to accelerate and then have to back off and recover. But in this situation efficiency is not the goal. What you want here is to make your opponent believe that he is hurting more than you are.

Perhaps the best way to play the psychological game with an opponent is to establish a little lead just before some obstacle, or a series of turns, a hill, a feed zone—anything that distracts. This was done expertly to me once while racing in Mexico. I was about 8 seconds behind another lone racer when we headed into a quarter-mile-long section of road construction. I could see him start to accelerate as he entered the gravel section. By the time I emerged at the other end, he had nearly doubled his advantage on me and I gave up the chase.

Another time I dusted off a solo rider who was bearing down on me with a similar move. I had about 10 seconds on him as we were going over a series of rolling hills. As I approached the crest of one, I accelerated and went all-out *downhill*. When he reached the bottom of the hill, I was much farther away. It discouraged him enough so that he was no longer intent on catching me, but just on finishing on his own.

Whether it demoralizes your opponent, or it just catches them off guard, it doesn't matter as long as you get rid of the unwelcome company.

Two on One: A Blessing, a Predicament, and Dealing with Both

I recall how a U.S. national team racer came to a coach and asked some very fundamental tactical questions—stuff that at first blush you would expect most anyone at such a level to know. Simply put, the rider wanted to know how two teammates in a breakaway can get away from a third breakaway companion.

Actually, it's not a bad question and riders should be prepared for that scenario, because if you aren't you might find the odd man out wins the race. Let's put it this way—the teammates back in the pack who were working so hard for the breakaway are not going to be very understanding.

YOU HAVE TWO

It really isn't such a rare thing to end up with a two-against-one scenario in racing. It happens frequently. If you're in a blessed situation where you and a teammate are away with one lone racer from another team, you must survey the situation:

How much lead do you have over the chasers?
How far is it to the finish line?
Will the lone racer work with you?

Your first concern is to maintain the break. A sure second and third place is probably better than the unknown finish that looms in returning to the pack. Because of that, evasive action against your breakaway companion isn't wise until you know that you, your teammate, or the three of you can make it all the way to the finish line. It really looks bad to start a silly cat-and-mouse game to lose the odd man, only to get caught by a charging field in the closing kilometer.

WHEN TO COOPERATE AND WHEN TO ATTACK

If the rider isn't working with you, first try to persuade him that it is also in *his* best interest to get to the finish line ahead of the pack. Once you've established a comfortable lead and the finish line is close enough for you or your teammate to solo in, start your attack. If the three of you are rotating, you might take a short pull at the front and then slip back to rest for a moment. Without being detected, slip off the back a few bike lengths (see Diagram 3.5) so you will have the advantage of surprise and greater speed when you blast by. Once your opponent has taken his pull, attack. If your breakaway competitor is at all interested in contesting the race, he'll jump after you. At this time, your teammate should be securely glued to the other racer's wheel (see Diagram 3.6). As the competitor chases, your teammate will get the benefit of his draft.

As soon as the racer closes the gap to you, your teammate should attack (see Diagram 3.7). It's again important for you to slip into the draft of your competitor. Be prepared to fire off a

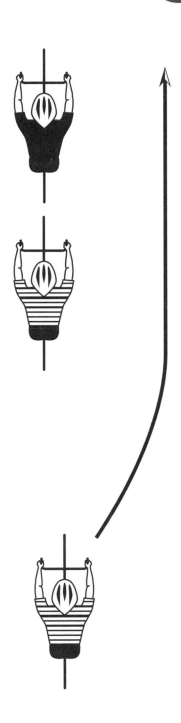

Diagram 3.5: Starting an attack in a two-on-one situation

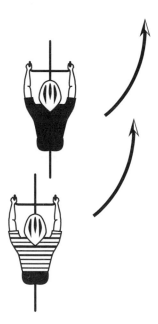

Diagram 3.6: A teammate can pull into the draft of the opponent as the opponent jumps in response to the attack.

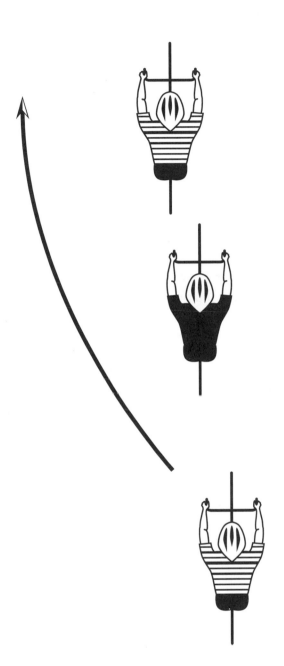

Diagram 3.7: When the opponent successfully closes the gap the teammate should attack.

few attacks in succession, because by now there is *no way* this guy will start pulling through with you again. Hopefully you can lose him and either you or your teammate will solo in to victory.

YOUR COMPANION IS JUST SITTING ON

What if the rider in question is simply not working with you? Maybe your breakaway competitor would rather see a field sprint and is trying to discourage your breakaway efforts. For example, on a flat stage of the Tour, you may see a teammate of Alessandro Petacchi or some other supersprinter slip into a break, but there is no way you will see this rider work to maintain the gap. The reasons are, of course, that the team wants to see the day end in a field sprint, so the rider is up front to monitor, perhaps to interfere, and finally, if the break succeeds, to launch his own attack while as rested as possible. This again needs evaluation:

> Is it going to be that bad for the racer to get a free ride?
> Is there some greater threat or situation that makes
> it necessary to pull ahead in another breakaway?

If it's time to ditch a racer who has just been sitting on your wheel, you will most likely have a harder time. It's most likely that he has been resting and he will be fresh. You probably won't be. Don't assume anything. In this case one of your riders,

Diagram 3.8: Ditching a rider who is sitting on

let's say it's you, should begin to rest a little bit more. Keep your pulls shorter than those of your teammate. Then, just a bit into one of your pulls at the front, launch your attack (see Diagram 3.8). If the lone rider has been sitting on throughout, he will be forced to go around your teammate to start chasing after you. Use approaching corners, blocking, or other interferences to your maximum advantage.

In all breakaway situations, you have to develop silent communication between you and your teammate. It's important that your teammate knows what you're thinking and planning. You might want to decide which one of you makes the first attack. If you're the stronger racer, you might want your teammate to make the first attack, tiring your competitor prior to your harder attack. Also, it's best if the rider who attacks does so when the competitor is most tired, after his pull.

YOU ARE THE LONE RIDER

It's usually no fun getting caught in a situation where you have no teammates in a three-up break. Just as in the converse situation, you must survey the situation.

How far is it to the finish?
What am I doing here, and what am I trying to accomplish?

You might be in a situation where there are teammates of yours up the road ahead of you or a teammate in the field behind you who you're working for—a sprinter perhaps. In those situations, don't pull. You are in position for a free ride. Have fun!

Maybe you've decided you'd like the breakaway to work and it's necessary for you to pull along with those racers. You put yourself in a compromising position because they outnumber you, but you're still committed to making the breakaway work. Maybe it's your best shot at placing. Be prepared for the attacks to come.

You also have some options if you have the strength and determination. Scope out the situation before the attacking happens. Try to formulate a plan. Is one of the teammates stronger? Does it look like only one of them has the strength to make it in solo? If so, you take advantage. When the weaker rider attacks, you can chase at less than 100 percent, ready for the counter by the stronger racer. Bluff. Sit up and let the weaker teammate go. If the other teammate gets nervous, you can probably figure he's now concerned that the two of you will get caught by the pack and the guy up the road won't make it to the finish line because he's not strong enough.

Here's another tactic to counter with. If the weaker racer attacks, you can jump after him in pursuit, but at less than your full effort. When you catch the weaker of the teammates according to standard procedure, the rider sitting on you now makes his attack. Respond instantly. When you catch him, they'll assume that you're ready for a rest. Don't stop—attack (see Diagram 3.9). If you opened up a gap on the racer who made the first jump, and that racer is tired, you now have both of them chasing you individually. Depending on your strength, and that of the weaker of the two teammates, you might elect to pull for a bit to polish them off.

Now What?

Your countertactics might produce several possible outcomes. First of all, the two teammates might reconsider their strategy, giving you more time to breathe and recover. You might change the landscape of the breakaway to a one-on-one situation, which is much more favorable for you.

Once you've neutralized one series of attacks from them, stop pulling in earnest, forcing them to do the majority of the work, if not all of it. In the latter case, it's now much harder to successfully lose you.

Variations on these techniques can be used in other situations and in larger breakaways. I hope that all of your future breakaways shake out in your favor.

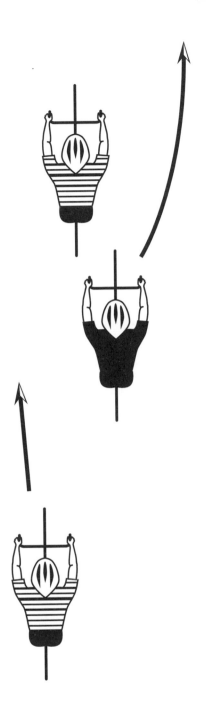

Diagram 3.9: Attacking a weaker racer when you are the lone rider

CHAPTER 4
Blocking: The Art of Being Uncooperative

Okay, so you aren't in the break, but you have teammates up the road. Here's your chance to assist in what could be a winning effort.

Though commonly used, the term "blocking" is probably not an apt phrase in cycling. Certainly, there is more to blocking than throwing your bike and body in front of a pack of chasing racers. In a sense, a more appropriate term would be "riding interference."

The first time some teammates and I tried to block in a road race, we took the term literally and that's about what it looked like. We were juniors training for the Canadian stage race and we knew very little about tactics. It was about halfway into a training race when one of our guys made his planned attack. The five of us left in the field massed at the front and literally created a roadblock. As I recall, the five of us were kind of weaving down the road trying to stop anyone from getting by to chase. It was very primitive . . . and it didn't work. As in this case, there's no sense blocking for someone if they can't keep the same pace as the pack.

To talk about blocking we must first establish that there are other cyclists to work with—teammates or friends. You must know how to block, even if you race completely solo.

First, if you're on your own in a race, you can watch the blocking (or lack of it) of the other teams and hopefully use that knowledge to your benefit. Secondly, you'll want to know what the other teams are doing to control the race. Knowing and seeing the team dynamics will again help you plan your strategy.

How to Block: This Isn't Football

Blocking should be tactful. Cycling is not a contact sport! In fact, very often the more subtle the block, the more effective it can be.

In a road race, blocking takes on certain styles and characteristics. Road races are generally longer, slower, and steadier events. There are few corners to string out the field of riders, and hills or crosswinds are often a determining factor. A breakaway of 15 seconds in a criterium is nearly out of sight. In a road race that same 15 seconds could mean a break is just dangling off the front, ready to be caught at any moment.

Blocking is not easy to do, either tactically or physically. The racers blocking will often get a harder workout than the teammate up the road. While the breakaway rider is riding at a hard pace, he or she is riding steadily. The blockers constantly have to make jumps and chase riders, close gaps, and fight their way to the front of the peloton. If a team is going to commit that much energy to a tactical effort, they have to know the strengths and limitations of the rider(s) off the front. Like my former junior teammate, who couldn't keep up the regular pace of the pack, don't waste energy on a rider who can't stay out there without accomplishing something. It might be a worthy accomplishment, however, if the racer you are blocking for can make the competition chase hard for a few miles. That might set up a counterattack by another team member.

So now you have a teammate away and it's time to block. Get to the front of the field. If you're going to slow the field down, that's the only place to do it.

The simplest way to block in a road race is to sit second man in the pack (see Diagram 4.1). When the first rider pulls off to allow you to pull through, swing off with him. This is very unnerving for the guy who has just pulled very hard and

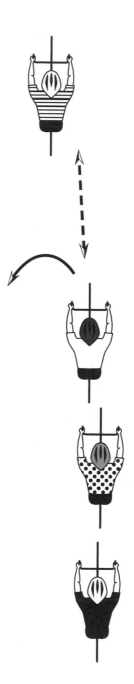

Diagram 4.1. Blocking

wants someone to pull through and continue his effort. This can cause a lot of dissension in the pace line.

The alternate technique is to soft-pedal when you pull through. That is, pull through but at a much slower pace than was established previously. The result will be very disruptive to the chase effort. Your soft pedaling will slow up the whole pace line and throw off its rhythm. You'll also be an obstacle, a block that the pace line has to maneuver around.

In both cases, effective blocking isn't accomplished by one turn at the front. As soon as you've made your small mark, you go right back to the front and do it again. You can go right back to the second spot of the pace line. Don't be surprised if no one is willing to let you in to the line this time. This is when it gets tough to be the blocker. You might have to slip, squeeze, force, bump, or fight your way back into the pace line to do any more blocking.

The Importance of Being Subtle

Subtle blocking—blocking without them knowing or realizing—is more effective when faced with a hostile pack.

The first time I saw this blocking technique, I didn't understand what was happening. There was this guy off the front of the pack, and his teammate was at the front pulling the pack up a long hill. It looked like one teammate chasing another down. Instead, the blocker, knowing his friend's strength, set a slightly slower pace up the hill than the breakaway. The pack was content to follow this pacesetter all the way up the hill, and the block was successful.

Sometimes one racer in the pack is strong enough to single-handedly reel in your breakaway or at least seriously cut the time gap. A blocking team needs to really watch for riders with that reputation and strength. If that guy hits the front of the pack, cover him; get on his wheel. Rather than sitting on his wheel and hoping he'll pull off sometime soon, it might be a better tactic to let him slowly pull away from you and open up a gap. One of a few things might happen—maybe he'll take a hard pull, figuring someone will pull through and match his effort—or instead, he'll find he's off the front and too tired to continue. Or maybe the gap you created will have to be closed by someone else wanting to chase. That's good for you, because now the second guy to chase is dead from closing the gap. Opening gaps like this is very disruptive to a chase.

Making the Assessment

Another possibility is for that strong racer to bridge the gap up to your teammate. With more strength, the break has a better chance of staying away. But letting one rider go off the front successfully encourages similar chases from the rest of the pack as well.

A racer blocking at the front of a pack has to make almost instantaneous decisions about whether he is going to chase, jump on the wheel of someone who is trying to chase, or let him slip off the front.

There are some key questions you have to ask yourself:

- Does the racer chasing have the strength to close the gap alone?
- What threat does this particular chaser pose?
- If this racer gets in the break, will it mean more strength and a better chance of overall success?
- Does the chasing racer have any teammates who will assist with blocking?
- What are the chances of the chasing racer reaching the breakaway and then going on to beat your teammate?
- Is the situation favorable to your objectives?

Two Against the Pack

Two teammates blocking in the field should keep a short distance apart from each other (see Diagram 4.2). One rider should be right at the front to either soft-pedal through the pace line or not pull through. The second racer should position himself in the fifth or sixth spot in line. Since most successful attack-type chases originate from about this far back in the pack, it's that rider's responsibility to cover the move.

When your team covers each move, it discourages additional chasing and it can set up another opportunity. Let's say that a really strong rider sprints off the front to catch your racer. You or one of your teammates covers the move, jumps on his wheel, and he makes it all the way across the

Diagram 4.2: The racer in front, A, can do the blocking while the rider in position B can watch for and cover attacks from behind.

gap. You now have a situation with two racers in the front group. When a team properly covers each chase effort, they'll always maintain a numerical superiority in the breakaway. Your team should position a racer in each new group of racers that join the lead.

From my own experience, I recall a classic example of how only a couple of racers from one team can control the entire pack. Once in the old Tour of Texas, my teammates Alan McCormack and Tom Broznowski established an early breakaway with several other racers on a flat, windswept 3-kilometer circuit. It was only in the final four laps that our team's blocking became critical, as their gap on the field started to dwindle in anticipation of the finish. Danny Van Haute and I were the only teammates left in a field that was chasing hard. We both got to the front of the crosswind echelons and soft-pedaled, opening up gaps in the pace line. As hard as we tried, the leaders' time hovered precariously around 25 seconds. Finally, as we hit a long crosswind stretch, I went right to the front and set a hard, steady pace. To those who didn't understand, it would actually look like I was chasing down my own teammates; instead, I had everyone pinned in the gutter trying to find a little draft from the racer they were following. Everyone was too tired from fighting the wind at that pace; they didn't attack. They were content with the pace I was setting. I knew that the pace was considerably slower than the pack would have averaged had they been allowed to continue with a crosswind echelon. Yet the pace I set was still slower than my two teammates away.

At the end of the crosswind, they'd added an additional 10 seconds to their buffer, but the long pull completely toasted my legs for the sprint to come. Of course, the important thing was Tom and Alan went on to finish first and second in that race.

To block is almost always to sacrifice. Hopefully, everyone on the team will have his or her day off the front.

CHAPTER 5
Wind, Hills,
and Other Challenges

Whether it's a blessing or a curse, I don't know, but for some reason, we don't have many races in the United States where there are serious crosswinds.

In one sense, it's a blessing because for some, when confronted with a crosswind, they get blown off the back of the pack. It's a curse for just the same reason.

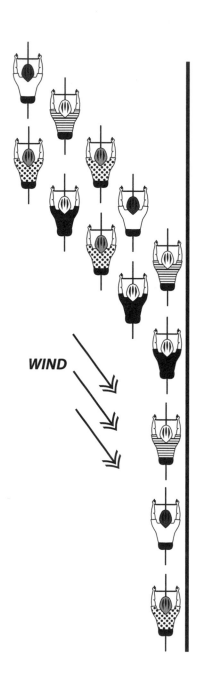

Diagram 5.1 · Effect of a crosswind on the back of the pack

In Europe crosswinds are about as common as short criterium courses are in the United States. As a result, everyone knows how to ride them. When a crosswind blows up during a domestic race, riders fight to get in the front echelon and then everyone struggles in the gutter until they get blown off or the wind changes direction (see Diagram 5.1).

Many years ago in the L.B.J. Ranch stage of the Tour of Texas, I made the mistake of assuming the pack would react like a domestic field, instead of the European one it actually was. The pack was heading directly into a strong headwind. I knew that the course was about to take a 90-degree turn to the right in a few miles, so I went right to the front in anticipation of the pack's reaction.

The front of the pack accelerated in a mad dash as we crested a hill and saw the corner ahead. I figured I was in a great position, turning the corner in the fourth spot. What I didn't anticipate was for the 7-Eleven riders to form an echelon of only four riders, keeping everyone pinned in the gutter. I made the mistake of continuing to try and get into the lead echelon. I was stuck out in the strong wind, fighting to hold onto the wheel in front of me. I was making a classic mistake. I should have moved all the way out to the left and started a second echelon.

Behind me, someone was doing just that. In a few moments they got organized and started to move. This group was moving so quickly and efficiently, they blew past

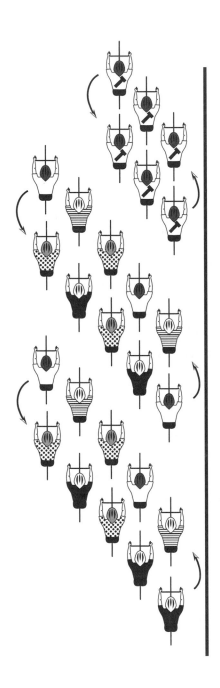

Diagram 5.2. In the European pro ranks, echelons will form one after another, down the road.

me. I further compounded my predicament by fighting the wind in the gutter to work my way into this echelon. I was now so tired from fighting the wind that I missed the next three echelons that went past me.

In Europe, as soon as the peloton hits the crosswind, the riders fight to get in the lead echelon; but the moment it's established they form another right behind, and then another right behind that (see Diagram 5.2). It goes on and on, echelons rotating down the road, one after another. Most of the sorting out of who is and isn't in the lead echelon takes place before the riders even hit the crosswind.

Probably the best recent example of a team taking advantage of the power of a crosswind was the U.S. Postal team's well-planned, and very coordinated effort in the twelfth stage of the 2003 Vuelta a España.

The peloton was powering its way into a strong headwind that day, but director Johann Bruyneel knew that at the 50 km-to-go mark a sharp right turn would put the field into a strong crosswind. Working for team leader Roberto Heras, the Postal squad massed at the front as the peloton hit the turn. The team roared across the bleak, treeless plains of Castilla–La Mancha. Strong winds were cracking from the left and the Posties' pace quickly blew the peloton into three groups.

Caught out of position were some big names, several of whom were vying for the overall lead, including Dario Frigo and defending champion Aïtor Gonzalez. Race leader Isidro

Nozal from ONCE made the jump, too, but the move turned the three-week stage race into a two-man contest . . . one that Heras won in the decisive time trial on the penultimate day of the Vuelta.

Getting in Position

The first thing you can do to prepare yourself for a crosswind situation is to check the prevailing winds in relation to the racecourse. Generally, the only time this information is valuable is in a road or circuit race. Always make sure you're at the front of the group when you hit a crosswind. You'll be positioned best for getting in the lead echelon—and, in this country, that might mean the only echelon—or the next one if you have to form it.

If you weren't prepared as the crosswind hit the field and now you're about to face fighting the crosswind alone and in the gutter, try and take some quick action. You can either try to start another echelon or work your way up to the lead one. Your decision has to be based on quick judgments. Are all the strong riders in the lead echelon? If so, forming a second one might mean conceding the race. If you think the level of tactical sophistication in the field is lacking, the rest of the racers may not respond to your attempts to form a second echelon. In this case, you must fight to get into the lead echelon. Before the effort of fighting the crosswind starts to tire you out, accelerate and move out toward the front of the echelon.

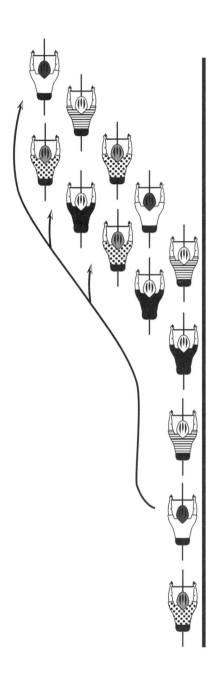

Diagram 5.3: Regaining position in a crosswind echelon

Look for a little opening. Try to sneak into the group via the "slow lane," or go all the way to the front and just create another spot for yourself (see Diagram 5.3).

If you decide the only logical thing to do is to start another echelon, slowly move across the roadway into the wind. If the rest of the riders sitting out in the wind aren't sure what you're doing, don't hesitate to tell them. Sometimes verbal encouragement (and verbal intimidation) is your only means of getting another group to form an echelon. I'll also warn you now, in the United States, "pack logic" prevails. Many times I've formed strong second echelons directly behind the lead one, working just as smoothly, only to have riders abandon it to fight the wind to get into the lead echelon (this is where some verbal chastising might do the other riders some good). The only place to be in a crosswind is to be working in an echelon. Don't fall victim to the common mistake of getting in the draft at the tail end of the echelon and expect to stay there. While it might be a nice place for a few hundred meters, you're likely to be squeezed out into the wind or even knocked down. Most accidents in echelons happen right at the tail end because some riders are fighting to get in, others are trying to rest, and some riders in the echelon are changing from the slow lane to the fast lane.

Staying In

Sometimes getting into the echelon is only half the battle. If there are still more riders wanting to get into the echelon, then you'll have to fight to get back in each time you drop back. This can be a battle for several reasons. First of all, you have to accelerate up to the faster lane speed, and you can only do this once your front wheel is completely past the rear wheel in front of you. Furthermore, the rider dropping back after you is actually in front of you momentarily and you have to squeeze past him (see Diagram 5.4).

If there's another rider fighting to get into the echelon, he'll most likely be positioned right at the edge of the road. He might accelerate into the position you were planning on taking. As you can see, it is easy to understand why there can be crashes at the tail end of the echelon.

To stay in an echelon that has too many riders waiting in the draft requires fighting for your place. This may force you to lean on a rider here or there, a situation where bike handling skills are critical. Unfortunately, no amount of instruction can prepare you for what you are likely to encounter when you actually have to fight for position. Consider yourself fore-warned—when riders are fighting for position in the echelon, it can get pretty rough, even cutthroat. Persevere! Once the echelon has sorted itself out and you've established your place, the ride gets pretty easy. The group works together and, hopefully, the fighting is over with at that point.

Teammates or Friends

There are a few ways to make things a little easier during the initial fight to get into and stay in the echelon. The best tactic

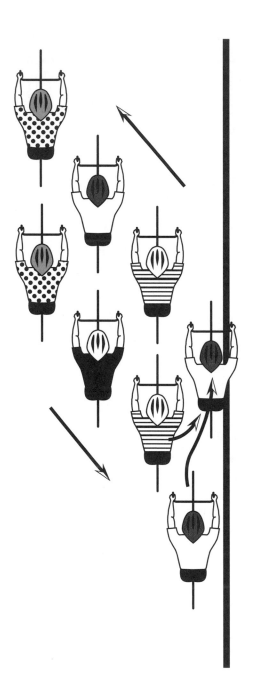

Diagram 6.4. Fighting to re-enter the echelon

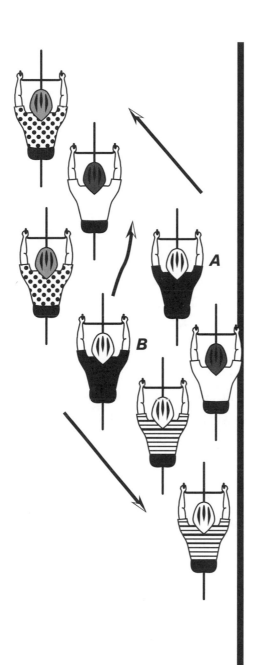

Diagram 5.5: Rider A allows his teammate rider B into the fast lane by opening up a small gap.

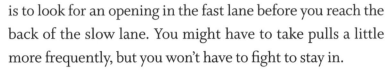
is to look for an opening in the fast lane before you reach the back of the slow lane. You might have to take pulls a little more frequently, but you won't have to fight to stay in.

If you have the strength for this tactic, you'll also make friends along the way. Everyone wants to be in an echelon with a rider who is willing to do more than his share of work. You'll stand a much better chance of getting room to maneuver into the fast lane. If you have a teammate or two in the echelon, you can work together and let each other into the fast lane before you reach the end of the slow lane (see Diagram 5.5). Your teammate who's already in the fast lane can let a little gap open up on the rider in front of him and let you accelerate into position.

If you have several team riders in an echelon you might want to do what Postal did at the Vuelta. Actually, here in the United States, the tactic would probably work to beat all but the most experienced fields. In any case, work with friends and teammates in an echelon so you can eliminate as much of the competition as possible.

In some crosswind situations you may find there's plenty of room for all of the riders in the group to stagger across the road; but some choose to sit on and not do any work. It'll be easy for those of you working to close the door on those sitting on. Simply shift the echelon downwind a bit so there is now only enough room in the echelon for those riders who are working. The riders trying to sit on will either be forced to work or forced into the gutter and then into the wind.

When Things Go Vertical

RACING HILLS

In road racing, climbs are the most likely places for the field to split. Either a group will break off the front or racers will slip off the back and get dropped.

Clearly, basic ability, VO$_2$max, and body type are the big factors when fields split apart. Still, there are a lot of riders who could be candidates for either group—those who get clear and establish a lead over a hill and those who are dropped. Those riders can better their chances of finding a spot in the lead group by understanding the dynamics of how a peloton breaks apart on a climb.

There's the obvious: a field starts up a climb and the stronger climbers make their way to the front of the pack. They force the pace and the peloton gets strung out. If the climb is long enough, the field can turn into one long string of racers. In order for this to happen the lead racers must work harder and go faster than the riders strung out behind them in single file.

Remember that once this thinning of the peloton takes place, a rider anywhere in the chain has to do just as much work as the riders at the very front. Since the benefit of drafting is so minimal with the slow speeds of climbing, following a wheel in front of you is more for keeping pace than anything else.

A tiring racer in the pack can easily become the weak link that can split the field.

REMAINING VIGILANT

A group of racers moves off the front or slips off the back. You can be caught on the wrong end of this split simply by not staying as close to the front of the pack as possible. When the whole field is at the edge of their cardiovascular limits, even small gaps created by fatigued racers can require a huge effort to close. The only way to avoid that is to always stay as far to the front of a group as possible.

It's been my experience that some of the most painful parts of a hilly race, when I'm tucked in the middle of the field, are not the long uphill grinds, but rather the transition of up, over, and down. Diagram 5.6 shows how a strung-out peloton, with racers linked wheel to wheel, can be torn apart as the lead racers crest the summit and start down a grade. While the racers in the back of the pack are still climbing the hill at 15 mph, the riders cresting the top are accelerating to 25 mph while the racers forcing the pace at the front are already speeding down the hill at, say, 40 mph. Something has to give and it's quite likely that somewhere in the middle, a weak racer is going to crack. Of course this situation doesn't apply to all hill climbs and, depending on the hills that you race on, it might not apply at all. But knowing this information can help you assess the group you find yourself in when the hills are rough.

Whether it keeps you from having to close gaps opened by weaker racers, or from needing to sprint over the top of a hill to stay in contact with the leaders, the safest spot on a hill is right near the front of the pack.

17 MPH **20 MPH** **27 MPH**

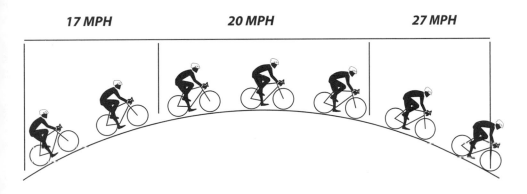

Diagram 5.6: Effect of hills on speed and the peloton

CHAPTER 6
The Importance
of Staying Informed

How many times have you been in a race with a breakaway down the road and you want to know how much time they have? You listen for spectators or your support crew to give you the current time split. Someone yells "22 seconds!"

Then you turn a corner and someone else yells "18 seconds!" Now you and I both know that over the course of 100 meters you didn't close a 4-second gap. The fact is you often have to discount the information spectators yell about the status of the breakaway. With all good intentions, they can be relaying erroneous time splits. Quite often people are calling out the time from the lead rider in the breakaway to the lead rider in the chase, or even to where you are positioned in the pack. Those aren't the time splits that matter to you.

What's important, and what you need to keep track of, is the time gap between the last rider in the group ahead and the first rider in your group. *That* is the time that matters the most, because when the lead rider in your group catches the last rider in the group ahead, the breakaway is neutralized.

The Wireless Peloton

Of course the advent of low-cost two-way radios have made this an easier task for any team. At the professional level, a savvy team director will keep his riders apprised of time gaps and other up-to-date information. Radios can also allow a director or a team captain to coordinate strategy on the road as the race unfolds.

My own experience with radios is mixed. They weren't a great presence during my racing career and my teammates and I learned to live without them. Now that they are a fact of life in the peloton, they are an integral part of race strategy.

In a road race, particularly one with a large peloton and accompanying caravan, the director's perspective on the race may be limited, so riders still have to depend on their own tactical insights as the race unfolds. I rue the day when we have a peloton full of riders waiting for orders to be barked into their earpieces before responding to a move.

Of course, the director—no matter where the team car sits in the caravan—is usually able to monitor race radio and send splits and other information ahead, even if he can't see everything going on in the peloton or the break ahead.

In a criterium, a director—or lacking a director or coach, a trusted friend—can offer pretty good insight by planting himself in one spot and radioing time gaps and other useful information to a rider (or riders) in the field. It may be a rider doesn't see that a serious competitor is lagging off the back, something the observer at the side of the course can see. In such situations, radioed information allows a rider to launch an attack to his advantage.

Chatter, Chatter, Chatter

One thing I will say about radios is that they can be as annoying as they can be helpful. I saw one really good example of that while following the peloton in Colorado's Saturn Classic—a brutal 134-mile race from Boulder to Breckenridge that includes more than 14,000 feet of climbing.

A break had developed early in the race and some team directors were on the radio from the moment the escapees left the field. After passing through Idaho Springs, and on the approach to the *hors categorie* climb up Guanella Pass, one director in particular was frantic and letting that emotion come through on the radio—much to the annoyance of his team. At one point, one of his riders in a chase group of twelve signaled for the officials' car to come up to him. The race commissar, knowing that the team car was well back behind the main field, correctly directed his driver to approach. As the car pulled alongside, the rider reached into his back pocket for his radio, pulled out his earpiece and handed the whole assembly to the commissar.

"What?" asked the confused race official. "Is it broken?"

"No," the rider responded, "no it ain't . . . but I have another 90 miles to go and I can't take it. . . . *You* listen to the silly sonofabitch all the way to Breckenridge if you want, but I'm not going to."

And with that, he was off.

Without Benefit of Radio

Even though they're cheap, not everyone has a radio, nor do they have someone to relay information. So rather than rely on radios or the Good Samaritans along the road, your best bet is to keep tabs on a breakaway yourself.

First you'll need a watch that can track seconds. Your cycle computer fills this role nicely. Of course, you'll have to still be in sight of the breakaway to do this.

Watch for the riders as they're approaching a corner or distinct marker, like the shadow of a big tree. With the clock reset to zero, start it the moment that final rider reaches the mark. When the first rider in your group reaches that same mark, either look at the time or stop the watch. If you're in a criterium, you can do a time check every lap or several laps. In a road race it's a good idea to do this about every mile, or as often as convenient. This information, along with all the other information you gather during the race, will supplement all that you know about the course and the competition and will help dictate your tactics.

Why Monitor?

By watch, cycle-computer, or radio, there are good reasons why you'll want to know the exact time gaps. The most obvious reason is so you'll know if the breakaway is gaining on you and your group or if you're reeling them in. This fact becomes even more important when you have teammates away in the break. In that case, you're going to want to make sure the time split stays the same or increases. If it's increasing and you and your teammates in the pack aren't doing too much work, you most likely don't want to do any additional blocking. Additional blocking may cause more concern in the pack and a more serious chase. Additional blocking would also tire you out more. If your teammate is pulling away, don't do any more work than necessary. Conversely, if you discover the time split to your teammate is decreasing, you'd better get to work, take some action, and block.

What's a safe amount of time between the breakaway and the chase? That's all relative. In a criterium, a 15-second lead can be insurmountable. In a road race, a breakaway with a 15-second lead might pack it in, considering themselves already caught. There are several reasons for this difference of perspective between road races and criteriums. There's a lot to be said for out of sight, out of mind. In a multi-cornered short course criterium, 15 seconds means the break is around the corner real fast. Since criteriums are often shorter and consequently faster races, the actual distance between the chasers and the leaders is usually much greater than in a slower-paced road race. Furthermore, in a road race the roadway rarely turns or twists often enough to get out of sight. An equivalent lead for a road race might be 45 seconds or more.

If you could have one basic plan of attack for criterium or road racing, it would be to make only one attack during the race and have it stick. Imagine if you could sit ten riders back in a race and then just when the winning breakaway was pulling away from the field, you'd attack and catch them. You wouldn't have made a dozen ill-fated attacks. You'd be in the winning break, and you'd be fresh.

Several top criterium racers do this quite successfully. It's really pretty simple if you have the speed that they possess. When they're sitting back ten or twenty racers from the front, they keep a close eye on what's going off the front of the pack. They'll watch each breakaway for the quality of the riders present and their time split. They also keep track of how fast the race is. Let's say the pack is averaging 29 mph toward the end of the event. They know from experience that they can't close a gap any bigger than 20 seconds when they go all out. If the pace is slower, they can afford to let the gap get a little bigger; if the speed is higher, they have to make their final move to the breakaway sooner. You only learn the limits of your ability in regards to this technique by trial and error during races and training rides.

Races so often follow the same pattern. There are many short, unsuccessful breakaways early on. As the race progresses, the breakaways open up a little more of a gap before getting hauled in. Finally, the right combination of racers hit the front. They open up a gap and it never gets closed.

Now, what if you're in the breakaway and you want to know how you're doing in relation to the chasers? Unfortunately, there really isn't any easy way to do that on your own. You can look back for an instant as you head into a corner on a criterium and check again the following lap. This will at least give you your relative progress. Another time you can safely take a quick look back is just after you've taken a pull and are dropping back. As you're just about to slip back into the back of the pace line, take a quick peek. You can get a rough idea what the time split is by starting your watch as you crest a rise or round a corner in a road race.

As soon as you or one of your breakaway companions sees the riders on one of their quick peeks, check the time. You can do this, but I feel it's a dangerous practice. First and foremost, you can end up wasting a lot of time and energy to see what your gap is. Don't bother to look around too much. It's better to keep your head down and work on getting the greatest lead possible. When you're in a breakaway, you'll probably have to rely on the information passed along to you from the side of the road.

Keeping track of the time splits will help you make decisions key to a successful race.

CHAPTER 7
Dealing with the Disasters

Catching the Group After a Flat or Crash

In bike racing, it's only a matter of time before something unpleasant happens and you find yourself off the back and chasing to reconnect. It's fortunate that in criteriums a free lap is now generously given by the officials for crashes and flat tires.

In road races, that just ain't gonna happen. If you're caught in a crash or suffer a flat, all the distance lost has to be made up on your own. If you're a lone rider, a cyclist without any

teammates to help out, the prospect of rejoining the peloton is pretty dim. Even with teammates, your chances can be pretty slim; but, if your team is organized and willing to do the work, and the situation makes an attempt possible, the process of chasing back on can be made to look simple.

I recall during one USPRO Championship race, a teammate of mine destroyed his front wheel and frame in a pothole. With a focused effort and teamwork, we managed to get him back into the field within just a few miles.

In Europe, rescuing team leaders off the back of the pack in road races is almost commonplace. I recall a particular incident at the Tour de France that illustrated this so clearly. One day the cameras caught a comical moment when former Tour winner Laurent Fignon crashed on a downhill corner and his bike flew off the road and was stuck in a tree. What struck me at that moment wasn't the serendipity of the bike landing in the tree—although I have to admit, that was kind of cool—it was the fact that the French cycling star didn't seem all that concerned about reconnecting with the group. He knew he could count on his teammates to help him back on.

Most domestic racing is different in that we don't have a moment to waste in beginning our chase. We don't have such long-distance races that allow plenty of time to rejoin the peloton, nor do we have the services of eight teammates, or that mile-long race caravan to draft our way through.

For you to bring a rider back from a flat or a crash, there are certain prerequisites. The pack has to be followed by support cars, either your team's or neutral support. You also need to have at least one other teammate to help you out.

When a crash happens, team members need to quickly find out who went down. If it's a rival, you may opt to attack. The same holds true for flat tires, except they can often be concealed from opponents (in the case of slow leaks) and changed before anyone knows differently.

Let's say that one of your teammates just went down in a pileup. You need to quickly assess the situation. Is he one of the stronger riders on the team? What's that rider's overall potential for the race? If the team is counting on that racer to do well at the end, or if he is the strongest rider on the team, or has the best chance to win or place high, an effort should be mounted to rescue him. On the other hand, if the rider who just went down was barely hanging on and his or her time in the field is limited, it would be a waste of energy to try and bring him back.

Now you have to assess the race situation. What's going on in the race? Is there time to get your teammate back into the field before the finish, before the next major climb, and so on? Is the pack speed slow enough that you'll be able to reconnect? If the answer to these questions is yes, then you need to act quickly.

Quick and Discreet

For our example we'll say that you have a four-man team. You must first notify your two other teammates that so-and-so is off the back and we need to get him back in the field. Don't go and shout at the top of your lungs, either. Roll up alongside and tell them discreetly. The last thing you want to do is let everyone else know that you have a racer off the back. Someone would likely attack just to make your life hard.

What happens now depends on the race situation and the team personnel. One rider, the strongest one left on the team with the greatest chance of doing well, goes to the front to try and slow things down and make it easier for the chase effort from behind (see Diagram 7.1). That way, should a breakaway start to develop, he's there to jump into it and represent the team. If no one else in the pack knows what's going on, so much the better. Make your actions inconspicuous.

The other two riders drop back to the back of the peloton. If the teammate suffered a flat tire and you know for a fact that a follow car has given him a new wheel, one of the riders drops off quickly to help the racer.

If the dropped racer suffered a crash or there's some doubt if a wheel change took place, both riders stay connected with the pack and don't drop off. A racer who crashed might not be able to get back on the bike; he could drop out of the race. It would add insult to injury for another teammate to drop off the back, only to have to chase on alone because there was no one back there to help. As a rule, the first rider doesn't drop off the peloton until word comes from a follow vehicle or race official that the rider in question has begun a chase. This is, of course, another case in which a radio can be a blessing. Either way, wait until you hear

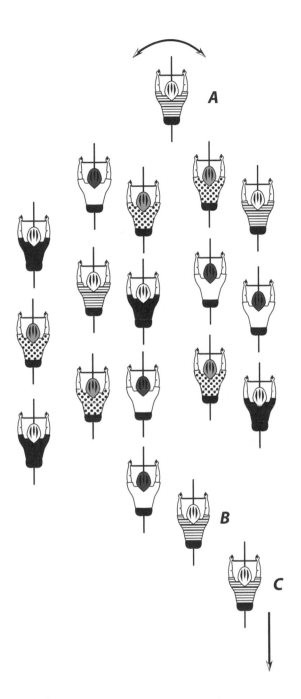

Diagram 7.1: Rider A goes to the front and tries to inconspicuously slow the field. Rider C drops off the start working with his teammate who had the flat. Rider B waits for the two to approach from the rear.

about the rider's condition and his potential to reconnect before sacrificing the chances of any more of your riders.

When a rider drops back, he has to do so quickly. There's no sense in having two guys off the back and not working together right away.

During a team time trial of a stage race, I suffered a puncture just a few miles into the 15-mile event. The team decided to wait for me as I got a wheel change; but they made the common mistake of "just pulling through easy" until I caught back on. Why waste time waiting for one rider going at 100 percent at, say, 27 mph just to catch up when the team could have dropped back and covered that same ground together at 32 mph? It would have been much more efficient to have the team sit up, hit the brakes, and roll along at 5 mph. Then all of us could have started right back in at full speed. As it happened in that event, when I caught my teammates, I was *dead* from the chase and had to sit in and recover for a few miles, further slowing the team. Don't make that mistake. Drop back quickly.

Now the two racers together off the back start working together like a team time trial. The chase needs to be an all-out effort to make up the distance as quickly as possible. The longer you're off the back, the greater chance there is of a major attack happening, a breakaway going, or the pace picking up.

The other teammate, sitting on the back of the pack, keeps a constant lookout for the two approaching from the rear. As soon as he sees his two teammates and sees that they are closing in on the peloton, he drops off to do the last bit of work to make contact (see Diagram 7.2).

There's always a great sigh of relief when the three riders finally make contact with the back of the field; but the danger isn't over yet. The rider who dropped off last has to tow his other two teammates all the way up the front of the pack. After chasing so hard and for so long, there's the tendency to want to sit at the back and take a rest, to recover. That's not a good idea (see Diagram 7.3).

Many years ago in the USPRO Championship, Tom Broznowski crashed hard. His teammates Michael Vaarten and Volker Diehl dropped off immediately to help him get back on. They did this because it was understood before the race that Vaarten, a track specialist, and Diehl, a criterium specialist, weren't going to be able to complete the full 156-mile distance. Any work they could do to help the team before they dropped out was their highest priority. As they appeared through the follow cars, I dropped back and towed Broznowski all the way to the front of the peloton. It was only then that my teammate could justifiably start resting.

Another story tells a hard-learned lesson. I was in the old Aspen Alpine Cup race in Colorado as a first-year senior. I got caught in a crash and had to chase and chase and chase. I was so relieved when I finally made contact with the back of the field. I sat right at the back completely exhausted but happy I was back on. A mile later there was a big attack and a hard chase at the front. I slipped off the back, too tired to hold a

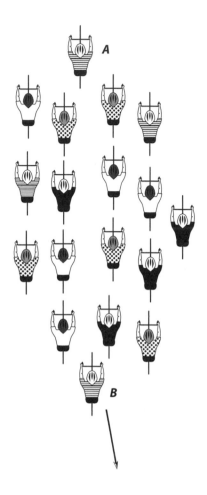

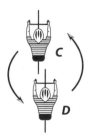

Diagram 7.2: Rider C and D work together and close the gap to the pack as quickly as possible. When rider B sees them approaching, he drops off to help with the final distance.

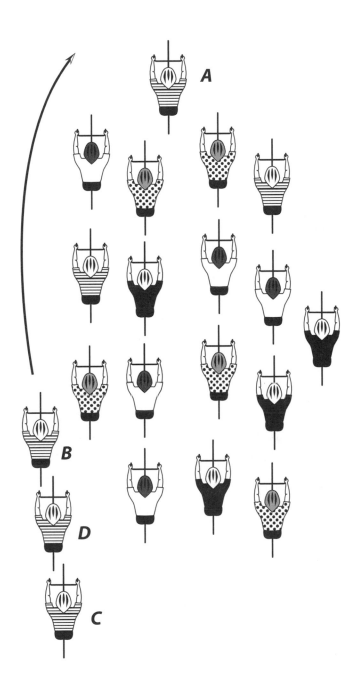

Diagram 7.3: Racer B brings the two teammates the final distance and continues to take them to the front of the pack. There, tired from chasing, the racers have a pack they could slip through if necessary.

wheel. This time I had nothing left to give to a chase. In retrospect, I would have been much better off farther up in the field when that attack came. I may have been just as tired, but would also have had to slip through the entire pack before getting dropped again. The pack is your buffer to recover.

A Little Planning

Before a road race there's no need to try and plan for every possible situation and scenario; but if there are a couple of key players on the team who figure to be your best shot, it would be wise to discuss how everyone would work together to get them back into the pack. Ideally, of the racers left in the pack, the strongest would go to the front and try and slow things down, to cover any attacks. The next strongest teammate would stay at the back and wait until the last moment to drop off and help his teammates back on. The team's weakest—the worker or domestique, if you will—would be the first rider to drop back and help the racer who flatted or crashed.

That's the *ideal* scenario; of course, things rarely work out that way. There would be little point in sending some rider off the back if he weren't up to the job of working to get back on. Maybe there were only three of you in the field to begin with. These are situations that might benefit from a few minutes' discussion before the race. Otherwise very quick decisions will have to be made in the pack as the situation develops.

CHAPTER 8
Tricks of the Trade

Resting during a Race

Often the difference between finishing in the middle of the pack and placing high—or even finishing with the pack or trailing in off the back—is a matter of how well you feel when the crunch comes, how fresh you're able to stay until the critical moment. This means staying fresh and resting *whenever* possible. And I do mean that: whenever possible!

Racing is an endless series of efforts and recoveries. The more you rest and recover, the more you'll have for the efforts. It's not just a matter of sucking a wheel until the critical moment, either. There are many times during a typical race when a smart rider can accomplish a given task and do so with a considerably lower expenditure of energy.

One of the points former national coach Eddie B. always tried to impress upon us was that riding a race was like working on a calculator. There are only a finite number of attacks or hard efforts you had in you during the course of a race, and each time you made a jump, bridged across to a breakaway, or sprinted for a prime, you had to deduct it from your total potential. This is true to a point. Of course, you can make attacks and recover, but there's a limit to your energy and how much work you can extract from your muscles. The point is to conserve your strength.

Be Smart

The best way to conserve is simply to be smart. Don't make a bunch of foolhardy moves and attacks. You don't want to be analyzing every pedal stroke, but you should have some purpose behind your moves. For one thing, you shouldn't be doing someone else's work for them. If it's really the responsibility of another team to chase down a breakaway, stay out of it and rest. You'll be fresher for the next attack.

Conserving little bits of energy adds up, too. For example, small tasks like moving to the front of the group may not require *much* effort, but multiplied over the course of a long race these moves begin to really wear on you.

Look for ways to conserve energy. Work with a teammate to chase down a breakaway or to get to the front of the pack. Sometimes it takes a supreme effort just to get to the front of the pack. Having a teammate there can mean the difference of staying there or slowly drifting back.

Slip-Sliding

One excellent way to conserve energy is to simply ride slower than the rest of the pack. Sure, we know that you can't do this for too long. You'll be off the back of the pack. But a little technique, which I call "slip-sliding," can be very effective for resting and recovering if done carefully.

On the Morgul-Bismarck stage of the Coors Classic nearly twenty years ago, I had a teammate really take advantage of the hills and the course to ride easier than the rest of the pack. Every time we reached the base of "The Wall"—a tough 14-percent grade that marked the end of each lap— this rider would be right at the front of the pack. He would start to lead up the hill at a slower pace than the rest of the field was willing to ride. By starting the climb at the front, he managed to slip back through the field so that, at the top of the hill, he was right near the end of the peloton. He was riding up the hill each time at a pace and effort level that was significantly lower than the rest of the riders, who kept pace with the lead riders going up the hill.

Each lap this rider—who I must qualify by saying was one of the best climbers in the race—would start at the front of the pack and then slip to the back of the pack. Over the course of several laps, he had expended significantly less energy than the rest of the field and when it came time for the "big crunch," he was still fresh and ready to go.

There are times you can use this technique and there are times you *have* to go just as hard as the leaders or be dropped. The key is to know just when to go hard and when to rest. While knowing exactly when to be at the front would be like gazing into a crystal ball, you can certainly make some reasonable assumptions. When the "heavy hitters" are sitting back in the pack and some less threatening racers are forcing the pace, you can figure it's relatively safe. In most races, there's a major climb or other obstacle, which can be the determining factor of the race. All of the other climbs and attacks are not critical.

Going *Up* the Down Staircase

After sliding to the back of the pack on a climb, you'll somehow need to regain your position near the front, if for no other reason than to repeat your earlier slide to the back. Rolling hills offer a great opportunity to do exactly that.

When sitting in the back of a group, you can take advantage of momentum to move to the front of the pack. It's important to understand the dynamics of how a pack descends. The riders at the front can never descend as fast as a racer sitting in a draft. There is a finite speed at which a rider breaking the wind can travel. We all know from experience that sitting in the draft going down a hill, we often have to feather the brakes to keep from riding into the wheel ahead of us. So, what better time to get to the front than when the pack is going downhill and you're using your body weight and momentum to move up?

Depending on how hard the pack is going, it may only take a little maneuvering to get to the front. If the peloton is tightly packed, it takes some real skill maneuvering safely through the pack on a descent.

There are only a few basic techniques to moving up on a descent. You have to start your assault on moving up by scoping out the pack and deciding on how best to get through the field. Look for openings. It's best to try and keep your options open as much as possible. I found it best to skip down the side of the pack going from one draft to another (see Diagram 8.1). If the side of the roadway is jammed, look for possible routes through the middle of the peloton that might offer an escape farther down the road. The idea is to be able to get the maximum benefit out of a descent.

On most hills—as long as the pack isn't blasting down—there's a spot at the end where you can really make up a tremendous amount of ground. What happens is that the lead riders in the pack might rotate on the descent to keep

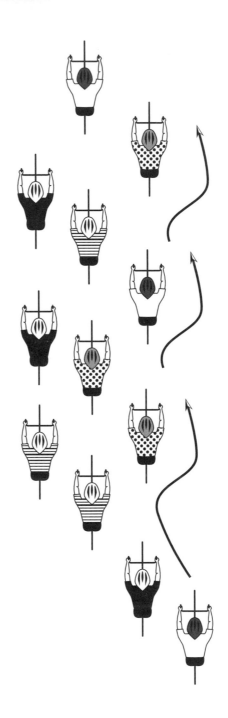

Diagram 8.1: Moving up on a descent

their speed high, but once the roadway levels off or starts to roll back uphill, there is often a noticeable lull at the front. Finished with the descent, riders who were up front slow down compared to the riders still coming off the hill and still in the draft.

Take advantage of the speed you have coming off the hill, even increasing it by tucking into a more aerodynamic position or accelerating into the draft of another racer right at the bottom of the hill. What you'll find is that with practice, you can sometimes build up enough momentum to go blasting by the front of the peloton.

Free Rides to the Front

Most racers go real fast, ease up a little, and then go hard again. This cycle continues for the entire race. There are times during the "big crunch" that you simply *have* to be at the front of the race. To do anything less than fight as hard as you can to get to the front would mean watching the race and maybe the winning breakaway go. Once there, you may well be able to sit in when the pace is going hard, wait a few minutes or miles until things cool off a bit, and then get to the front with a lot less effort.

Whenever you can get towed to the front of the pack, you should take advantage of it. When you know it's time for you to get to the front of the pack, drift to the side of the peloton and watch for racers coming up the side from the back and heading

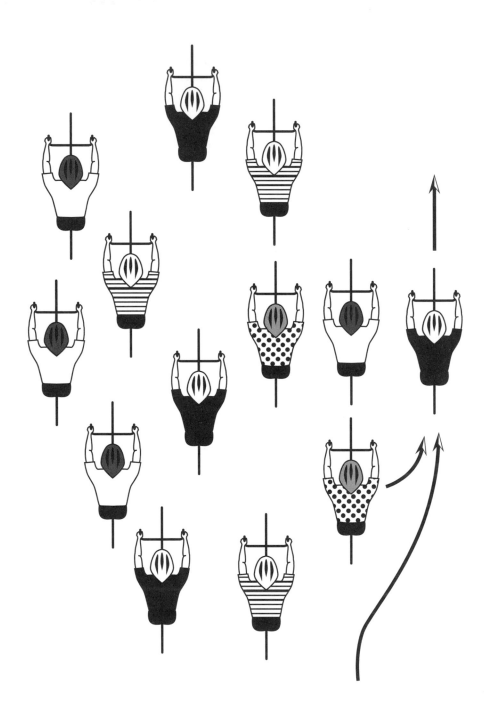

Diagram 8.2: Looking for a "free ride" to the front of the peloton

to the front. Slip in right behind them and take a free ride to the front (see Diagram 8.2).

Sometimes you can get all the way to the front without having to go out into the wind at all. Of course, the faster the pace is, the more important this technique is for saving energy. As a general rule, whenever you're in a fast or difficult race you should jump on these free rides to the front. It's a good habit to get into. Maybe you've been in a race where it seems like you have to continually pass riders just to maintain position. Slipping back in the pack can be an excellent energy-saving technique. You can play off the rolling hills and zoom back to the front of the pack when there's a lull after a downhill. Waiting for a rider to jump behind on his way to the front of the pack can save some energy.

A Word of Caution

These are all great energy-saving techniques, but you mustn't get too carried away with them if your objective is to finish in the lead, off the front, or to win the race. Yes, you need to save energy; but you have to know when to rest and when to go hard.

There are times, as you learn from experience, where you have to go hard—that "big crunch" we talked about—and saving energy then is no savings at all. That rider I was telling you about who used the "slip-sliding" technique perfectly at one Morgul–Bismarck stage is a great example.

Maybe he became too enamored with the technique, because the following year he drifted to the back as we headed up "the wall" one too many laps. As he was sliding back on one trip up the hill, the winning break took off and we were never able to catch it.

Turning the Tables

Every once in a while you see a tactical maneuver orchestrated with such stunning brilliance that it ranks as poetry in motion.

If you know what's happening in the race without others realizing what's happening, you have to have a great deal of appreciation . . . *even* when the move is against you. It may be frustrating, but at least you have a degree of appreciation for it.

There was one of those moments in my own career. Maybe what I saw was insignificant. Maybe it didn't have any bearing on what happened at the end of the race. Maybe the move wasn't even intentional. But it was nonetheless *brilliant*. It showed me how two individuals can turn the tables against two of the strongest teams in a race and change our team's function from one of blocking and frustrating the field's efforts, to one of us chasing after our own riders.

This is just one example of how the tables can be turned and a few individuals can counter a large squad. Obviously there were a lot of circumstances that created this situation, and they may never appear like this to you for as long as you race. But fundamentals of this maneuver can be applicable in many situations you encounter. Watch for them and try to turn the tables on the other guys.

Before I explain what happened, I have to explain the race situation.

We were about halfway through a national class level criterium race. The course was a tight 0.6 mile with six turns. Only the start/finish stretch was wide or long enough to make any continued chase or advancement in the field. The back-stretch had a succession of corners that strung out the field into single file.

As expected from a course this tight, a small group got away. Three riders broke clear of the peloton and the field was brought to a virtual standstill. The riders were Dan Franger from Alfa-Romeo, Tom Broznowski from Schwinn, and Tom Schuler from the 7-Eleven squad. Each of the strongest teams had riders represented in the breakaway, and now all of their strong teammates were going to slow the pace and ensure their advantage.

Within a few laps, the break's lead had increased substantially. The field was not *about* to simply give up. There were still many strong individuals and small teams anxious to chase. One of the strongest and fastest riders in the field was Shaun Wallace from Great Britain.

Even though Wallace raced without the support of a team, he rode very well, mostly on sheer ability and talent. He's also a smart racer and makes friends in the pack. He'll often enlist the support of other independents for their common benefit. In this race, he was overwhelmed 14 to 1. Wisely, he didn't try and chase the break initially. He made full-blown attacks alone to try and bridge the gap to the leaders. He was hoping that slow reactions from Schwinn, Alfa-Romeo, or 7-Eleven would give him a little gap, and we would let him close the rest of the distance to the breakaway alone. This would have worked to his favor, and then he could have taken advantage of the eleven riders in the pack designated to block for their teammates.

It would have been a big mistake for any of our teams to allow that to happen, because Wallace has a very fast finish and he could easily have won the race. That would have been an embarrassment for the three most powerful teams in the race to block for a breakaway and then none of their racers wins from the break!

In the early stages of the breakaway, Shaun, with his incredible speed, closed about half the distance to the leaders in a lap-and-a-half attack before he ran out of steam. After each of his efforts, the time gap quickly climbed back to where it was before. Wallace needed help. He dropped back in the pack and found someone else who was upset with the turn of events in the race and had the ability to help.

The next attacks were combined efforts. Wallace would attack with his enlistment on his wheel and after a lap at breakneck speed, the next rider would pull through. One of these might have worked to bring in the breakaway earlier, but now the time gap was too great. It was going to take several attacks like this.

Now came the little move that still sticks in my mind. Like I said, I don't know if Shaun really planned this or if it was done out of frustration, but the effect was still remarkable.

Wallace had just taken one of his flat-out, one-lap pulls and swung off, going into the backstretch with its succession of corners. Pulling through at nearly the same tempo was one of his enlistments (I don't recall who it was). Sitting second was a 7-Eleven rider. Shaun slipped in front of me going into the second corner. As we approached the third corner, Wallace eased up on the pace. Because of the succession of corners, I couldn't move around him until we reached the fifth turn. It was as if Wallace was blocking, taking a "divide-and-conquer" approach to bike racing. (See Diagram 8.3.)

Wallace knew that even though 7-Eleven, Schwinn, and Alfa-Romeo were working together for their teammates, there was an underlying fierce rivalry. I couldn't let Wallace's enlistee and the 7-Eleven racer get up the road. I had to chase these two riders. Had the 7-Eleven rider known what was going on behind him sooner, he might have turned from blocking to pulling in order to catch the break.

I was forced to change modes from blocker to chaser instantly. It took a lap of all-out effort on my part to reel

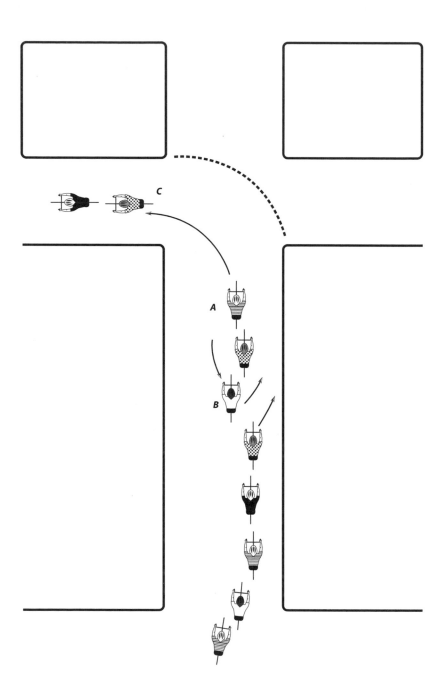

Diagram 8.3: Shaun Wallace pulls off the front (A), and then moves in front of me (B). Wallace slows me down, allowing the two lead riders to open up a gap (C) on the field.

back these two. It was brilliant. And if Wallace had been fresher or there had been another comrade of his sitting on my wheel, another attack would have followed.

I was irritated and delighted at the same time as I pulled at the front of the pack.

A tactical maneuver like this has to be executed perfectly and only under the right circumstances. It would have worked wonderfully if Wallace had let his enlistee and a Schwinn and Alfa-Romeo guy off the front, too, because there's no way that 7-Eleven could allow the balance of the breakaway to swing out of their favor and toward their archrivals. This would only work if you knew for certain that the team left behind was going to chase, or that the enlistee was a teammate that could represent you well in the breakaway.

As a postscript to this tactical discussion, Wallace's combined efforts were just moments too late. The three riders, whose lead was more than 30 seconds at one point, finished the race in front of the pack, but only by a second or two. It looked more like Franger won a field sprint than a breakaway sprint. Not unlike intense rivals, the Schwinn, 7-Eleven, and Alfa-Romeo riders stopped working together in the last couple of laps and started jockeying for position, unwilling to tow the others to the finish line.

CHAPTER 9
Time to Sprint:
The Charge to the Line

Since we are talking about staging a lead-out, we assume that you will have at least one other racer to work with, as that's the whole idea. One—and preferably more—racers work together to lead out another racer for a sprint. If you don't have any teammates or friends to employ this tactic with, simply knowing the process will enable you to take advantage of other teams as they work to lead out their sprinter.

First, let's look at the underlying principles of a lead-out (see Diagrams 9.1 and 9.2). If one racer is leading out another for a prime, it means the racer giving the lead-out is sacrificing himself or herself for the following racer, presumably one who has the better chance of winning the prime. If the following racer, the designated sprinter, can uncork a blistering 150-meter sprint, the lead-out rider "should" drop him off 150 meters before the finish line. In order to do this, the lead-out rider will probably have to work close to maximum effort for 200 to 700 meters before the 150-meter mark. This ensures his sprinter is right on the front of the pack for the final 150 meters. This is how it is *supposed* to work.

Now, let's throw in a team lead-out situation with a strong field challenging to win the race. This is what a lead-out is really all about, as shown in the following illustration.

During his phenomenal racing career, Davis Phinney won more bike races in the United States than any other pro, not only because of his tenacious sprint, but also for the lead-out efforts of strong teammates like Ron Kiefel. He would not have won nearly as many races otherwise, as it was those lead-outs that enabled Davis to be in the right place at the right time, specifically, the second rider about 200 meters from the line.

Lead-outs can be simple half-lap exercises with one rider leading out, or they can be elaborate, planned, orchestrated, and precisely executed team efforts with half a dozen riders stringing out the pack for the last several miles. The finishing

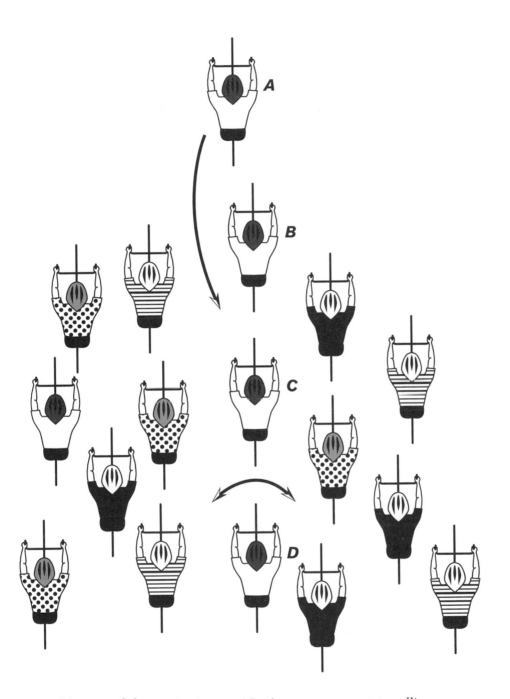

Diagram 9.1: A and B (or more) lead-out men may rotate pulling for rider C (the designated sprinter) up until the final 150 meters. Rider D is the sweeper, responsible for keeping the riders off of the designated sprinter's wheel.

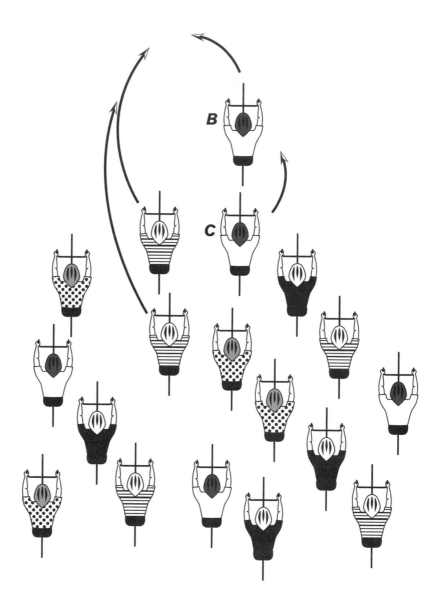

Diagram 9.2: In the final lead-out, the sprinter C "drives" the final lead-out rider B. In this illustration a wave of riders on the left threatens to swarm past and close down the lead-out. The lead-out rider can halt the threat by easing over left and not giving them open road. The sprinter would accelerate to the right side and escape before getting boxed in. All of this must happen prior to the final 200 meters where they must ride in a straight line.

"trains" of Mario Cipollini's Saeco and Domina Vacanze squads, or Fassa Bortolo's long and coordinated lead-outs for Allesandro Petacchi are examples of such team efforts.

Lead-outs in their finest form—as you see in the opening weeks of the Giro d'Italia or the Tour de France—can be beautiful to watch. In situations where many top professionals are competing for such high stakes, it is quite normal for several team trains to be working at the same time to set up their top sprinters. Team trains often drag race each other to the finish line. Strength and a great deal of skill keep the lead-out from derailing.

I have a good, albeit "ancient," example from my own career of how a team can plan, execute, falter, and then recover during a lead-out effort. We were to race in Borrego Springs, California, and our manager let us know right away that he didn't care what we did *during* the race as long as we won the final sprint.

The plan sounded simple enough. Everyone on the team was to meet at the front of the pack with ten one-mile laps to go, and that is when the lead-out was to begin. Jeff Pierce, Tom Broznowski, Steve Speaks, Chris Huber, Danny Van Haute, and I were to keep the pace so fast for the final 10 miles that no one could attack, so our teammate, Mark Whitehead, could have a clean shot at the finish line. Another teammate, Gibby Hatton, was to sit on Whitehead's wheel to keep any other good sprinters from taking advantage of our lead-out. Hatton was the "sweeper," effectively sweeping the sprinters off Whitehead's wheel.

Even with the collective strength of our riders, a 10-mile lead-out was pretty ambitious and nearly a wasted effort. During a pace line lead-out, you always have to save a bit of energy while pulling into the wind, for fighting your way back into the pace line. The exception is if you are making your last pull before the finish line.

In our case, the lead-out began well enough. Each of the riders rotated at the front, pulling, keeping the pace so fast that no one else could make a serious attack. But after 8 miles of a 30-plus mph pace, our lead-out started to fall apart at the most critical time. Anything a lead-out accomplishes prior to the final sprint is really insignificant. What matters most is getting your designated sprinter to the final 150–200-meter mark at the front of the pack.

By the end of our lead-out, all of us (including myself) pulled off the front too tired to make the extra effort to fight the charging peloton for our position back in the pace line. Once that happens, the rider is swallowed by the pack and getting back into the pace line is nearly impossible.

With one lap remaining, we were down to only Van Haute and me working for Whitehead. This would have been fine had we not already pulled so hard for 10 miles. In the final effort of a lead-out, the sprinter directs his teammates in front, telling them to move to the right or left, pull longer or harder. The sprinter is in a better position to watch what is happening in the pack and might be threatening to the lead-out. The sprinter is driving the lead-out racers. If the pack is starting to swarm past on the left side, the sprinter can move his riders to the left and shut down the "wave," which could swarm across the lead-out.

In situations like this, the sprinter may have to really bark out instructions to the leading racers, or teammates have to quickly pass on information to the front of the lead-out. (In Whitehead's case, anyone who knows him *knows* that shouting has never been much of a problem.)

My final pull, directed by Whitehead, was for half a lap. This length would usually be much too long leading up to the final sprint, but, short of teammates, that was what was required. Van Haute finished the now tattered lead-out to the last turn, about 200 meters before the line.

We won the race, but barely. Looking back, we had little reason to celebrate. We blew it tactically and won only because we lucked out. Against slightly better competition, or facing another team organizing a lead-out, we would have certainly lost and wasted the whole effort. The important lesson to remember is not to start the lead-out so early that you have nothing left when it really counts—as you approach the finish line.

In the closing kilometer or two of a race, a pack can surge from left to right in waves. These waves can come swarming up from behind with anxious racers intent on the finish line. If a group of racers moves across your lead-out, you will be boxed in. That can be one of the most frustrating experiences: You're ready to sprint like a madman but you have *nowhere* to go because you are surrounded by slower competitors.

What to Do Without Any Teammates

If you're smart, you can consistently place in the front of a field sprint by following lead-out attempts of other teams or individuals. By following the moves of the designated sprinter, you can take advantage of the lead-out. This isn't a trade secret. Just watch the riders fight for Mario Cipollini's wheel as a 200-rider peloton surges to the finish. At least in the early part of the 2003 Giro d'Italia it almost seemed that Allesandro Petacchi's favorite lead-out man was Super Mario.

If you have a well-known sprinter in your field, the obvious problem is that there will be several other riders fighting for the same wheel that you want. That gets very tricky and downright dangerous at times.

If staying right on the sprinter's wheel is not possible, the next best thing would be to stay right near the front of the pack, but on someone else's wheel. When the last lead-out man hits the front for the sprint, try to move in behind the sprinter.

Again, you may have to move someone off his wheel to do this. And if the lead-out effort is not well coordinated, you might even try to take the place of the sprinter on the final lead-out man. You would be surprised at how often the final lead-out is inadvertently given to a competitor from another team. This is understandable, given the harried and panicked atmosphere of a field sprint.

Practice lead-outs whenever you can, or try to take advantage of other team and individual lead-outs. They are difficult to master, and any experience will be of tremendous benefit. Practicing them in training is not at all the same as executing one smoothly in a race situation. In review:

- There has to be at least one person to lead out the sprinter.
- The final lead-out person has to drop off the sprinter at 150–200 to the finish line.
- In a pace line lead-out save some energy to get back into the pace line.
- Watch for "waves" that could get you or your teammate boxed in.
- The sprinter directs the lead-out.

The Final Effort: Throwing Your Bike at the Line

In 1984, history's first Olympic road race for women came down to a final sprint between American teammates Connie Carpenter and Rebecca Twigg.

The winning margin was only an inch or two, so close that neither woman really knew the outcome until the slow-motion video was replayed on TV. What made the difference, and gave the win to Carpenter, occurred just an instant before the finish. On the film, you could see the two racers approach the line handlebar-to-handlebar and then, about 8 feet from the line, Connie's bike lurched forward. It was the finishing touch of a good sprint polished golden. She "threw" her bike at the line.

Throwing the bike just before you cross the finish line is an all-important technique. It's a technique that wins countless races. It decided more than a handful of races in 2003, when Allesandro Petacchi went on his historic hunt for stage wins in all three grand tours, often beating great sprinters like Mario Cipollini and Erik Zabel by mere millimeters. A speedy sprint without an effective throw at the end could turn an otherwise perfect effort into something less than victory. Throwing your bike at the finish line doesn't always mean you have to be going for the race win. Throwing your bike in a close pack sprint can mean the difference between sixth or fifth, tenth or eleventh. As long as there's a photo-finish camera, you'll get the better place as a result of throwing your bike and passing one of your competitors at the line.

I recall a sprint finish between Roy Knickman and Roberto Gaggioli at the Reno stage of the Coors Classic. It's a great example of what seemed like a close sprint at the time, but looked quite different on film.

In the photo Knickman and Gaggioli were both throwing their bikes at the line. It was as close to a tie as you can get. If you were to measure the photofinish image with a ruler you would find that Gaggioli won by the width of his front tire. This race was won by the throw of the bike. That's not to say that Roy didn't throw his bike. He did. He threw it almost flawlessly, but perhaps just a second too late.

Now, the technique. First, I'll say that you should practice throwing your bike anytime you practice a sprint. The only way you'll be able to successfully employ it is when it becomes second nature. The basic principle is pretty simple. It really is *throwing* your bike. The execution is what is critical and more difficult.

Diagram 9.3 shows how to execute this maneuver in most sprints. As you enter a sprint, you usually get out of the saddle for the jump (A). As you're accelerating, you stay out of the saddle throwing your bike from side to side. You'd usually do this in all but a windup sprint where the acceleration is gradual and there's no sudden burst of speed. Once you've made the initial acceleration, sit down and start to wind out the gear (B). It's natural to slide forward to the tip of the saddle as you're spinning the gear (C). This is when you're set up to throw your bike at the right instant, just before the line.

This is when timing means everything and where practice makes perfect. Throwing the bike boils down to one pedal stroke as you're positioned over the tip of the saddle, elbows cocked out. This pedal stroke is the last pedal stroke before the line.

In a sprint, you have a great deal of momentum and speed driving forward. Now, like lunging at the finish line, you have one final thrust. This thrust is captured in one-half of a pedal stroke—the right or left pedal, it doesn't matter. About 8 to 10 feet from the line, with your crank arm in the eleven o'clock position, you push the handlebars forward as you begin the last half-pedal stroke (D). Since it's the front of the wheel breaking through the plane of the finish line that counts, the bike is pushing forward, sacrificing your body's forward momentum. The finish of the throw is executed with the final push on the pedal, ending the stroke with the crank arm in the seven o'clock position—thrusting your arms forward, hyper-extending them, dropping your head, and sliding all the way to the back or even off the end of the saddle (E). All of this has to be done in a single explosive motion at the end of a sprint, and timed so that the final thrust happens just as your front wheel crosses the finish line.

How far you actually scoot to the back or even off the end of the saddle depends on the technique you develop. I've seen riders who throw their bikes so hard, they end up with the saddle on their stomach. It's probably not necessary to go to that extreme. In fact, it could be dangerous. I recall being taken down in a sprint when a rider threw his bike

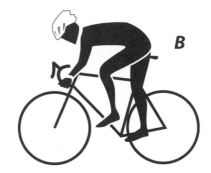

Diagram 9.3: Throwing your bike at the line

wildly after the finish line and lost control. His timing was bad and his technique was way off.

What has to be practiced is the actual throw of the bike and the timing of the throw so that your hyperextension happens right at the line. If you throw the bike too early, you'll have stopped pedaling before you cross the line. If you throw the bike too late, you'll still be pedaling and accelerating after you've passed the finish line.

In practice, you don't have to be sprinting at full speed to work on the technique. You can go through the same final steps at slower speeds. This will help as you learn the synchronization of the actual throw. This will be helpful because when you're just getting the hang of throwing the bike, it's tough to do that many all-out sprints. To put it all together, you will have to be sprinting at 100 percent. Otherwise, the timing will be all wrong.

Throwing the bike won a gold medal for Connie Carpenter in 1984. It won the Reno criterium stage of the Coors Classic for Roberto Gaggioli and it added to Petacchi's impressive score from 2003. With enough practice, it may do wonders for your placing as well.

CHAPTER 10
The Criterium:
A Tactical Microcosm

There's a fine art to riding a criterium. Probably more than any other situation—except team events on the track—criteriums require the greatest amount of skill and finesse to truly be ridden successfully. The reason technique is so important in criterium racing is that there are so many elements that can hinder your effort, like an aggressive pack of competitors and corners every several hundred meters.

Four or more corners a lap make the physical demands of a race that much greater. Now you not only have to respond to every attack, but you have to jump out of every corner just to stay with the wheel in front of you. Saving energy and riding as efficiently as possible is a big part of correct criterium technique. It's difficult to get to the final lap of a race at the front of the pack. Arriving there fresh or wasted can have a great bearing on when you cross the finish line. It's necessary to look at the criterium and evaluate it for ways to save energy and increase efficiency.

It doesn't take a racer long to see that if he doesn't continually work to maintain position in the pack, he'll soon be at the *back* of it. A top criterium racer once put it this way: "It's pretty simple. In a really hard criterium, for every racer that passes me, I try and pass five. If I do that, I figure I won't lose any ground in the pack." With all of your competitors in a criterium pack trying to get to the front, maintaining your place in the pack really means being able to move up in the pack. That can be accomplished with a great deal of effort, or with graceful ease. Now, if you want to be more than pack filler, you're going to have to get really good at moving efficiently through the field in a criterium.

The first thing you have to learn is when to go hard and when to take it easy. You can pull out into the wind and slug your way up five or ten spots, or you can wait for the opportune time and pass that many and more with much less effort. All races have their moments when the pace is blazing and then other times when the tempo settles down for a moment. Say you're in 20th spot and want to move up. Why not sit in the draft until that momentary lull in the pace (provided the race isn't taking off down the road without you) before accelerating to the front?

Equally as important as waiting for the right moment to make a move to pass riders, you should find the correct spots on the criterium course to make the moves to the front. The most obvious spots where you can make up some places in the field (or lose them) are the corners. The first technique would be to attempt to slow as little as possible through the corners. Simply put, don't brake as much. If you carry a fraction more speed through the corner than your competitors, you won't have to accelerate as much out of the corner. If the amount of energy seems insignificant, add up that fraction for four corners in each of fifty laps. It adds up big time. What this technique also means is you have to feel comfortable with your bike handling skills so you can ride up on the rear wheels of the racers in front of you, or squeeze your front wheel between the racers' rear wheels (see Diagram 10.1).

Where you take the corner in the pack, either on the inside or on the outside, can have a significant impact on how fast and efficiently you get through it. There are no hard rules here. During the race, you should try taking

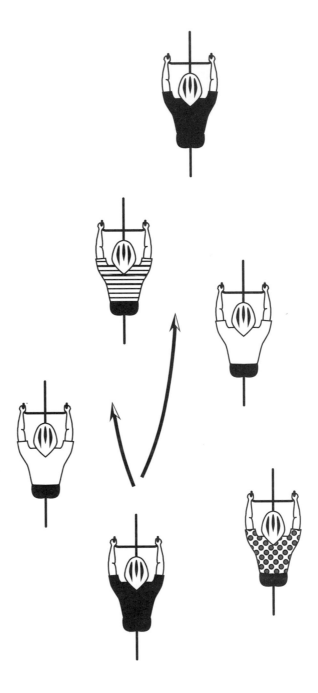

Diagram 10.1: Tactics for passing on a criterium course

different corners in different positions, first on the inside and then on the outside. Often, you can find a rhythm or a line through a corner that no one else sees and uses.

In a particularly competitive criterium in Southern California, I was having a difficult time holding my position through this one corner. I'd fight through the lap to move up three or four places and then I'd lose it all in that one corner. Everyone was diving for the same line and I didn't want to risk it. I looked for a different line though the corner. On the far outside, where no one was riding, I found the right spot. I approached the corner on the outside of the pack and did not slow down as everyone dove in to the corner (see Diagram 10.2). I kept riding straight for a few more feet before making the turn. I avoided the crunch and didn't have to brake as much for the corner. Suddenly, I was making up three or more places each lap in the same spot.

This story illustrates a lesson and a valuable technique for criterium racing—try to discover your weakness and attack that. This might mean something as simple as following a really good bike handler around the course to learn their technique or something as involved as learning to spin a gear out so you don't lose ground on the straightaways.

The other thing it brings up is the discussion as to when to fight for position and when it's not worth it. I'm sure you've seen plenty of times, as I have, when someone fights for a spot around a corner or in the pack as if it were for a $500

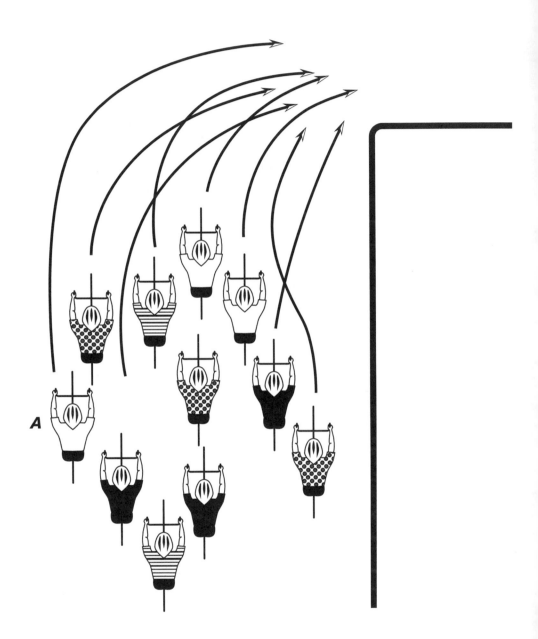

Diagram 10.2: If rider A can find a different line through the corner it could save time and energy and ultimately earn him a better position in the pack.

prime when they are 40 or 60 places back in the pack. No, you don't want to give up places in the pack, but keep it in perspective. What's the point of fighting for 63rd spot with thirty-seven laps to go and chance falling? Letting a rider in front of you now and again really isn't a bad idea. If you do someone this favor, they might be in the position of letting you into the pace line when you need it. You want to fight for position when you're at the front and something is coming up—like a prime, the finish, or a specific tactical move.

One of the oldest criterium techniques is blasting up the side of the pack as all of the riders are lining up to negotiate the corner (see Diagram 10.3). It's very effective for moving up many spots and it's also very annoying to the rest of the pack. If you try using this technique, I'd recommend you do it sparingly and don't be surprised if someone pulls out in front of you and shuts you down.

Another trick is to figure out how the pack is going to flow and sweep across the roadway and take advantage of it. What typically happens when the pack is starting to gear up for the finish is that the riders in the front will jockey for position. They will surge and then ease for a moment so as not to tire before a prime, final sprint, or lead-out. If the road is wide enough, the pack will also drift from one side of the road to the other. This ebb and flow can either work for or against you. If you're a little too far back in the pack, you can take advantage of this marvel and move up to the

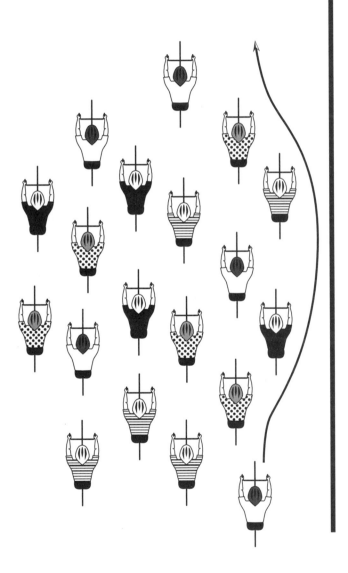

Diagram 10.3: Moving up the inside of the pack heading into a corner

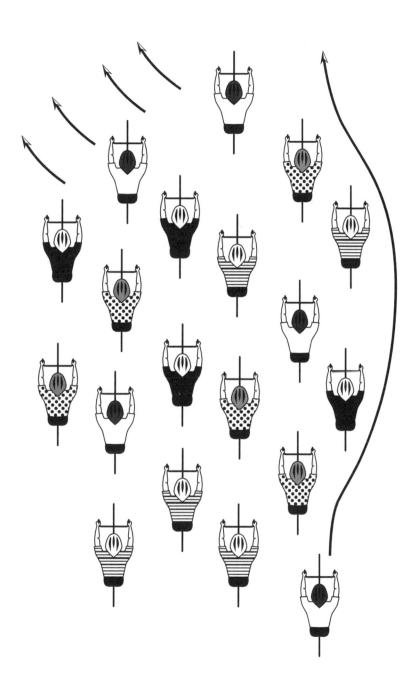

Diagram 10.4: When the pack is preparing for the finish, it is possible to move to the front by taking advantage of the changing speeds and the movement from side to side.

front of the pack in one quick move. Conversely, if you don't watch out, you can lose 20 or 30 places in the distance of 100 meters.

When you want to move up, the trick is to be positioned near the side of the field so when the field sweeps to the side, you can sprint to the front (see Diagram 10.4). When you know you're positioned poorly in the field and you have to move up like this, don't take any chances. When the pace slows, move all the way to the front. A common mistake is to move only partially up before heading for the wind protection of the group. When you do this, there's a good chance that the pack is going to sweep back the other way and you'll lose all of those places again.

To avoid being caught by the sweeps that occur, simply stay right near the front. If a wave of riders starts to swarm past you from one side, you can react and stay in front of them. When you're four or five riders back, you're at the mercy of the riders in front of you.

When you're warming up for the race, you should mentally rehearse just where you want to be in the field at each spot heading into the final sprint. This'll help you get a clear perspective on just what it takes to place high in a race. You can't expect to do well in a field sprint finish when you wait until the last lap to start moving up.

If you think the ideal position out of the last corner—which is 600 meters from the finish line—is in third place, you have

to plan backward from there. That means you'll want to be at least in the top five with two corners to go. With two laps to go, you'll probably want to be in the top ten. Since you want to be as rested as possible heading into the final charge, you should be right at the front with about eight laps to go. With ten laps to go, you should make those last major efforts to move from the center of the pack to the front.

If you go through this mental exercise before the race as you're riding around the course, you'll have a much better chance of being where you want when it really matters.

CHAPTER 11
Stage Races

If you like the tactical game of a single-event bike race, you'll *love* stage racing. The physical and tactical contest builds from stage to stage, with more and more factors coming into play. Strength, endurance, speed, perseverance, tactical wit, consistency, and luck all play a part in the outcome of the stage race.

Knowing when to go hard and when to take it easy is key to riding tactically in any race. In a stage race it's much the same as a one-day race, except that those same questions are spread out over several days instead of a few hours. Efficiency, conservation of energy, and recovery are critical to successful stage racing. Some very good bike racers make terrible stage racers because they can't recover from a hard ride soon enough to be a factor in the next stage. Other riders excel for precisely that reason and grow even stronger as the race progresses.

Planning

In a stage race, planning your efforts takes on strategic importance. Few riders can afford to make indiscriminate attacks and aggressive moves. The game is played out over the course of several days and several stages that offer a variety of tactical opportunities. You can plan an event around a particular course that might play to your strengths.

Before a stage race, you should take some time and think of some specific goals for the event. If you're serious about your goals, write them down. Looking back on these goals will be a real benefit when you're in the middle of the race and all you can think about are your aching legs and tired body. In that weakened state, it's easy to forget what you wanted to accomplish and end up settling for less than what you're capable of.

Your team should sit down and discuss team objectives and strategies. At such meetings, it's extremely helpful to be able to speak with authority about the actual racecourses. The strategy of the whole stage race might be based around one difficult stage. A long road race might not yield any opportunities to gain time on the field if it's flat as a pancake, but a 50-mile criterium stage situated on the side of a steep slope could determine the entire race. In your pre-race team strategy meetings, you need to think about and discuss:

- The demands of the racecourse, terrain, distances, rest time between stages, number of stages, etc.
- Your strengths and weaknesses.
- How quickly you recover from a hard effort.
- The strengths and weaknesses of your competition.
- Realistic goals.
- Optional plans (perhaps going for stage victories if a top G.C. placing doesn't work out).

Review the demands of each stage and assess your individual and team strengths and weaknesses. This should help you plan your efforts.

In any race, you must always be cognizant of the energy you're expending. In a stage race, it's even more critical. You can't afford to be making frivolous moves off the front or indiscriminately chasing down racers. While each stage will have its individual race tactics, you need to keep your overall stage race goals in mind. Plan your moves. Plan your efforts. If you're after a high general classification placing, you'll want to make your biggest efforts when they'll count for the most. Typically, that would mean putting in your hardest efforts during a time trial where every second is critical and in the most difficult stage where time gaps between racers will further split the field.

One of the things I like about stage racing is the complexity of a host of tactical maneuvers going on at the same time. There are races within the race. There's the overall general classification that is most important, but each stage also represents a race. In many races, there are king-of-the-mountain, sprint, and team classifications to work for. Going after one or more of the classifications takes planning and coordination with teammates.

Tortoise or Hare?

Former national coach Eddie B. used to advise us to start a long stage race as easy as possible by conserving our energy. In the second half of the stage race, we were to then pour on the steam. As long as one rider or team doesn't run away with the race in the early stages, this tactic can often work. This tactic is similar to the strategy employed by the patient criterium racer who sits back at the start of the race when everyone is blasting away at the front. Three-fourths of the way into the race, when everyone is exhausted, he easily jumps away. I've seen the Europeans use this slow start strategy successfully several times. After several days of hard racing, the European teams would make their serious attacks and build up big leads. You have to be careful if you employ this tactic—don't sit back so much in the first days that you lose so much time you can't get back into the action. Two years in a row I won the "Most Improved Rider" award at the Coors Classic. They gave the award to the rider who moved up the most in general classification over the course of the event. I'd always start off fairly easy and ride into the event, picking up fitness and strength as the event progressed. My G.C. after the prologue was *way* down the ladder. By the end of the race, I'd have moved past most of my competition.

Keeping the Accountant Happy

Another point Eddie B. always stressed during stage races was our limited energy reserves. He'd say it was as if there was an accountant keeping track of how many times we attacked. We only had but so many attacks or jumps in our legs, so we had better use them wisely. Take it easy in a stage race whenever you possibly can. This doesn't mean that you have to sit at the back of the pack—we know that can sometimes be more work. Rest before particularly hard stages. Don't kill yourself to save a few seconds on one stage, only to lose several minutes on the next because you're so blown out.

Make plans according to your strengths. If you're a really good sprinter, maybe you can capture time bonuses, primes, and stage wins. On the hilly road stages, where you know you'll get dropped, you might want to find a steady group of riders and spend the day with them, sharing the pace and losing as little time as possible. On the other hand, if you're a strong hill climber you might want to try and sit in on a criterium, resting as much as possible without getting dropped. The next road stage, you'll be fresh to make your major effort of the event.

It takes planning to be a successful stage racer. After you have done all of the physical training, do a little mental planning to make it pay off.

There's a lot to go after in a stage race. Pick something and go for it.

CHAPTER 12
Honing Your Skills:
Bike, Mind, and Body

Learning to Corner

Despite being fearsome climbers, a young Colombian team had its hands full at the Coors Classic one year. It wasn't the altitude or the steep grades of the Colorado stage race that presented a problem—the Colombians were prepared for those aspects of the race. However, the team was completely annihilated in the opening criterium.

Within ten laps the entire team was dropped, and by the end of the race we were lapping them like they were standing still. They'd never experienced anything like an American criterium race. The South American racers weren't used to cornering as fast as the rest of the pack.

It can be very intimidating to jump into a criterium and try to hang with the group if you're not used to going that fast and leaning that hard around a corner. By the final criterium of the stage race, none of the Colombians were dropped because they couldn't corner as fast as the rest of the field. How did they learn to corner with the best, and how do you learn? It'll take you more than a week and a half since you're not in a stage race, but you need to go about it the same way.

You learn by emulating the best. In bike racing, that can mean following the best riders. You'll learn real fast how you're doing because every corner is a test and the results are immediate. If you don't corner as well as they do, you end up chasing them down the next straightaway.

CORNERING BASICS

Of course there are some basics. When you corner, you have to keep your inside pedal in the up position so you don't scrape a pedal and crash. You only have to experience this once and you'll not forget—it's pretty scary.

Lean your body more than your bike. That's necessary for a few reasons. First of all, if you lean your bike too much your tires will lose traction and you'll spill. Leaning also lowers your center of gravity on the bike and makes you more stable. You can get very good control with slight movements of the upper body. All of this takes practice.

The two final elements of cornering are braking and taking the proper line. Experience is the best way to really learn braking and how to find the proper line through a corner. Just as the Colombians did, you should get in behind an experienced racer and try and stay with him or her as they go around each corner.

Watch the line the racer takes and follow in the path of his tires. Keep the distance between his rear wheel and your front wheel constant. That will mean you'll have to mimic their braking. Lean as they lean into the corner, and when they start to pedal you should start to pedal.

There are of course instances when you might not be able to do the exact cornering technique. This is when the seemingly subtle differences in bicycle frame geometry make a difference. A bike with shallow angles and greater fork rake will not handle as nicely and will want to drift out on the racer as he corners hard. A low bottom bracket might also make it difficult to pedal as much going into or out of a corner.

ULTIMATE CORNERING

Remember the first rule you learned about cornering—don't pedal through a corner and always keep the inside pedal in the up position. For what I call ultimate cornering you have to throw this rule out the window.

I really didn't become aware of this technique until just a few years ago. I was watching Davis Phinney setting up for a corner in one of those one-lap time trials that they held before the Wheat Thins races. I had already ridden and knew how fast you could go around each corner. Well, I thought I knew how fast until Davis hit the corner. I couldn't believe it. He never stopped pedaling around the entire turn! Granted he almost lost it when his rear wheel skipped sideways a few inches in the middle of the turn, but I had to stop pedaling for several seconds through the hardest part of the corner.

The next time I experienced firsthand how much faster you could corner was during a breakaway with Roy Knickman at the Reno stage of the Coors Classic. We were both going as hard as we could with only a couple of laps to go and we held a slim lead over the field. I got behind Roy on a corner and he would take a bike-length-and-a-half lead on me. After pulling for all I was worth at the front, I now had to close a gap on my breakaway partner out of the corner. As we went into the next corner I made sure I kept up all of my speed and didn't brake. We came out of the corner and he still had a bike length on me! The next corner I really watched him and saw how he was pedaling all the way through the corner. I managed, through sheer panic each corner, to stay with Roy. If we weren't going fast enough through the corners, I now had to pedal to stay up with him.

This technique is extremely difficult to master. It will take practice, practice, practice, and a lot of guts on your part. Before you ever attempt this technique, you have to have reached the stage of bike handling proficiency so that you're able to handle hitting a pedal in a corner without falling. You have to be at a level of expertise so that your only option for getting around the course any faster is to take two or three more pedal strokes on each corner when everyone else is coasting. That is the *only* time that you will need this technique. For goodness' sake, don't use this technique in the middle of a pack. It's not going to do you any good and you're only endangering the skin of everyone else should you make a mistake and fall.

The best time to use this ultimate cornering technique is when you're off the front in a breakaway where speed on the corners is critical to success or failure. You can use it to catch a breakaway or catch back on after a crash, a flat tire, and so on. If you're like Davis, you could also use it to lead the pack into the last turn of a criterium to get a little gap going into the sprint. That's risky, though!

The technique is simple in principle. You approach the corner in the same fashion, and the line leading into it is the same. Brake as needed while going into the corner, and start to lean just as you would for any other corner, but you continue to pedal. As your inside pedal starts to reach parallel to the ground, gently rock the handlebars outward, bringing the bike to a more upright position. As you continue to pedal, and your inside pedal becomes perpendicular to the ground, rock the bike further upright so the pedal just clears the pavement. Finish out the pedal stroke by gently rocking the bike back over to its normal cornering lean before starting over again with the next downstroke of the inside pedal. This allows you to keep your speed up all the way through the corner and exit the corner with more velocity.

Practice, practice, practice, and a lot of nerve. I recommend that you find a deserted parking lot to first try this technique out. Before this will be successful, the amount of lean that you can accomplish before a pedal hits the pavement has to become second nature to you. Practicing and applying these techniques make it critical for you to always train and race on the same bike with similar wheels. A change from clinchers to tubulars from practice to race will render the practice of finding that delicate lean useless. Missing the angle of lean on the corner a degree can spell disaster if you hit your pedal at the wrong spot on the road.

Practice, practice, practice, and be careful.

Bike Handling Drills

Good bike handling is a combination of natural ability and a set of developed skills. Nothing can prepare you for all that

will happen in racing situations. Still, regardless of what natural ability you start with, you must still encounter situations and experience them to learn how to react and to develop a natural instinct for reaction.

First of all, bike handling skills are essential. The rider who doesn't know how to handle his bike doesn't belong in a pack. He endangers himself and the lives and limbs of other competitors. Most everyone can learn and benefit from bike handling drills. Some things are natural, like maintaining your balance. Other techniques—like proper crash technique—can run contrary to first instinct and must be "relearned" for cycling.

I must say that I approach this whole subject of bike handling very seriously and, above all, cautiously. The drills I am about to describe are dangerous. My warning shouldn't be taken casually. The discussion focuses on trying to *avoid* crashing and then respond properly if you do go down. Bicycle racing is dangerous and crashing is inevitable. I've learned most of my bike handling skills the hard way—by falling in races. I hope that these drills help you and perhaps even prevent you from falling in a race or while training.

There's some irony here because as I make that statement I must also say that you are *very* likely to fall while doing these drills. Let's hope not; but it's better to fall when you're expecting it, than to fall *unexpectedly* in training or racing. Franklin Roosevelt once said, "The only thing we have to fear is fear itself." Okay, I admit that he was talking about the Great Depression, but a bike racer, too, can learn a good lesson from old FDR.

I figure that more people crash because of their *fear* of crashing than they do from downright uncontrollable situations. By now, if you've raced for even a short while, you've undoubtedly seen crashes in races that, in turn, trigger new crashes when riders simply overreact to the sights and sounds of the other crash. It happens all the time. Certainly you never want to discard good judgment, but don't let your fear rule you.

Since most racers are thrown into pretty frightening situations in every race, we should differentiate between unwarranted fear and legitimate danger. Of course, you'll have less fear when you're more confident with your bike handling, so let's move on.

TUMBLING

Before you learn how to avoid falling, you must first learn the proper way to fall. In bicycle racing, there are usually two types of falls. One type frequently happens in a corner. Tires lose traction, a tire rolls, and so on. Most often in these situations, you fall on your side and slide. These types of falls aren't fun, but they are usually not a serious matter.

The other type of crash occurs when a rider hits something (or someone) in the road. The racer goes over his or her handlebars. These situations are far more serious. For these extremely dangerous falls, we want to practice tumbling routines until they become second nature. They must become second nature, because it's a perfectly natural instinct for a rider who's flying over the handlebars to try and stay upright. This is the worst thing you can do. Your injuries will be much worse. You must learn to tumble—to tuck and roll instinctively—the instant the crash happens.

Find a gymnasium with mats on the floor or a soft, grassy field to do this drill. After a warm-up and some stretching (until you are nice and loose), start off with a few little tumbles. Simply squat down, put your hands on the mat, tuck your head and roll over onto one shoulder and then onto your back, just as you used to do in your grade-school physical education class. After some practice, increase the height on the tumbles until you're actually jumping over a low vaulting box or a training partner or two.

There's nothing wrong with using your hands to help break your fall. The danger and potential for a broken wrist or collarbone arises if you *lock* your arm to brace for the fall. The arm should only be used to lessen the impact. If you tuck your head correctly, your bent arms can absorb some of the shock before your shoulder blades take the impact.

I've seen racers stay upright as they fly over the handlebars, and the results are painful. They quickly let go of the handlebars and throw their arms out in a locked position to break the fall with their head up. With this response broken or jammed wrists or a broken collarbone are much more likely. And because the arms still can't break the velocity of the fall, riders hit the pavement with their face first, which also brings about tragic consequences.

Practice these tuck and roll tumbles until they become automatic. With this tumbling routine, you learn to instinctively tuck and roll so that when you hit something with your front wheel and fly over the handlebars, the proper reaction is your natural reflex.

BUMPING

Given that we love a sport where we ride at high speeds, shoulder-to-shoulder with 30 to 200 other people, we are bound to bump into a few of them more often than not.

Despite the fact that it is common, bumping can be very frightening—and, if you don't know how to react, it can also be very dangerous. It really doesn't take much practice to turn a potentially dangerous bump in training or racing into an incident hardly worth mentioning. The person who goes out of his way to bump into people gets the feel for how it should be handled. This is exactly what I propose you do.

Find a willing training partner of similar bike handling abilities. First, you need to convince him or her that you're not out of your mind. Point out that the drill might just save you both some skin in the future.

Find a nice, grassy field void of sand spurs, broken glass, or other objects that might puncture a tire, or worse, your skin.

This is where you'll start your drills. Wear gloves and your helmet for safety purposes. You might even want to wear tights to protect against grass burns when you fall.

Notice I said *when* you fall. For this drill, the fall shouldn't be any worse than not being able to get your feet out of the pedals at a traffic light. The speeds you'll do these drills at will be very slow. All you want to do is get the feel for what it's like when someone leans on you in a race.

Before you begin, let's review some important factors for safe bike handling. First and foremost, your arms *must* be bent. Stiff arms cause more crashes than perhaps anything else.

The shoulders should be loose as well. Bent arms and a relaxed upper body absorb shock—road vibration, potholes and bumps on the handlebars, shoulders and arms from other racers—much like the suspension on a mountain bike responds to hazards in the trail.

Start off riding side by side at a pace just fast enough to maintain a straight line. Now, move together and touch elbows. After you feel comfortable with that, one of you should lean your shoulder into your partner's shoulder.

Please, at this point, *never* do any maneuver like this without making your partner fully aware of what you will be doing. Don't suddenly crash into his shoulder without him knowing about it in advance. You might knock him down (and that's another drill).

When you are both comfortable with what you've been doing, the two of you should lean into one another and ride across the field. Notice how the handlebars respond and how the bike handles when you maintain a relaxed upper body. Now, try a slow ride across the field with stiff arms and locked elbows. The difference is remarkable and, in cycling, downright critical.

As you become comfortable with having someone lean on you while you ride, you'll want to start really bumping shoulders and elbows like it might happen in a race. *Do not* try bumping handlebars; there is nothing there to absorb the shock when you hit someone with your handlebars. All of the impact goes into turning the front wheel, usually causing a fall.

The simple idea behind these drills is to get you to understand how the bike responds when someone bumps into you while training or racing. Admittedly, a grassy field isn't going to give you a precise feel of what it's like to be bumped while riding on the road—but then again, it also won't give you the precise feel of what it's like to hit the deck and that's one element of realism you want to avoid.

When you feel completely comfortable with these drills on grass, you can graduate to a deserted parking lot for a few mild bumps of the shoulders or elbows; don't try anything too ballistic with hard pavement below you. These drills will prepare you, as much as possible, for what will likely happen when you get into tighter racing situations. By knowing how it feels, by knowing what to expect and how to react, you'll feel safer, ride more safely and, perhaps most importantly, not *over*react.

TOUCHING WHEELS

Accidentally bumping into someone's rear wheel is perhaps the most common cause of accidents in bicycle racing. Depending on how the incident occurs, even the most experienced bike handler is likely to fall. The touching or bumping of wheels I'm referring to happens when a rider overlaps his front wheel with the rear wheel of the racer in front.

Here's the typical sequence of events that occurs when someone touches a wheel on his or her right-hand side (see Diagram 12.1).

1. One or both of the racers move, so the wheels touch.
2. The front wheel turns left, away from the impact, pivoting with the headset.
3. With the wheel turning to the left, the racer has to lean to the left to maintain balance and ride away from the rear wheel.
4. From the moment the contact is made, the rider is forced off balance. His weight is actually being pushed to the right and into the wheel.
5. He then tries to compensate for being off balance by turning his handlebars into the rear wheel.
6. The rider falls over the rear wheel.

This sequence is the result of the body's natural tendency to compensate for being off balance. However, the fact that you

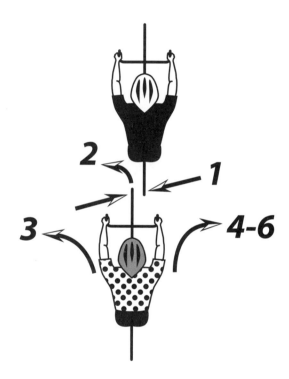

Diagram 12.1: Typical sequence of events when a rider touches or bumps the rear wheel of another rider

have two gyroscopes (a.k.a. "wheels") attached to your bike makes the natural reaction the wrong one. What it takes is a little practice to learn a new set of natural responses. The following drills will help prepare you to handle those encounters when you brush wheels. If nothing else, these drills will illustrate how dangerous it is to get yourself into those situations where you do overlap wheels.

I strongly recommend this first drill for anyone who'll be racing in any mass-start event. Although I don't have the data to back it up, my personal experience suggests that most crashes occur because of overlapping wheels—and many of those occur right at the start of a race.

In a typical road race, the moment the official says, "GO!" everyone takes about two pedal strokes and tries to clip into their second pedals. Virtually every member of the field is looking down at that moment, weaving down the road at 5 mph. It's inevitable that sooner or later someone overlaps a wheel and falls.

TOUCHING WHEELS DRILL

Find a grassy field and one other training partner to practice this drill. As always, you should wear a helmet and, for this particular drill, you might want to wear regular shoes rather than cleats. You'll be putting your feet down on the ground in a hurry and won't want them locked into any pedals. In addition, your equipment could take a beating from these drills, so try to use old tires and wheels if you have them. Have your partner ride at a pace just fast enough to maintain a straight line, which should be at about walking pace.

Ride up behind your partner and overlap your wheel. Now, turn gradually into his rear wheel and try to maintain your balance as the wheels make contact. Put your foot down before you lose total control and fall to the ground. Try this a few times from each side to understand the dynamics described above. If nothing else, you'll see how dangerous these situations are and avoid getting caught in them while training and racing.

Now try the drill a little differently. This time just brush the wheel momentarily. At a faster speed, about 7 to 10 mph, ride close to your partner with your front wheel overlapped on his rear. Now move to within 3 to 5 inches, and quickly turn your wheel toward and then away from the rear wheel. You may have to try this a few times before you actually make contact with his rear wheel.

The idea is to just tap the wheel and maintain control of your bike. Continue this several times until you feel more comfortable with how the bike handles. This part of the drill is designed to ease your fear about touching wheels. Like many aspects of bike handling, the worst thing to do is overreact.

You should never try intentionally touching wheels while riding on the road. There's too great a chance of error and a fall.

WHEN TO WORRY

The best way to keep from falling over someone's rear wheel is to avoid circumstances and situations where it might happen. As I said, the start of a race is frequently a scene in which this sort of accident occurs with some regularity. Try to be aware of that fact and play it safe.

Beyond that, you need to watch your front wheel in relation to everyone's rear wheel. Of course there are innumerable times during which you will be overlapping wheels. It is impossible to race without doing so. When you're in a potentially dangerous situation and you know it, you can be ready to react. There are other times when you should be quite safe overlapping wheels.

You're in danger when you overlap a wheel and the racer in front of you could potentially move quickly into your front wheel. This generally happens at the front and near the edges of a peloton and especially in a crosswind echelon where someone is likely to make a quick move to the side for an attack (see Diagram 12.2).

A safe racer isn't going to intentionally swerve and take your front wheel out from under you. There's also a chance that the racer in front of you might go down or get his wheel crunched. These incidents may occur when the racer in front doesn't know that you are following off to the side.

If you do have to closely follow a racer and overlap wheels, tap your brakes a few times and call out and signal that

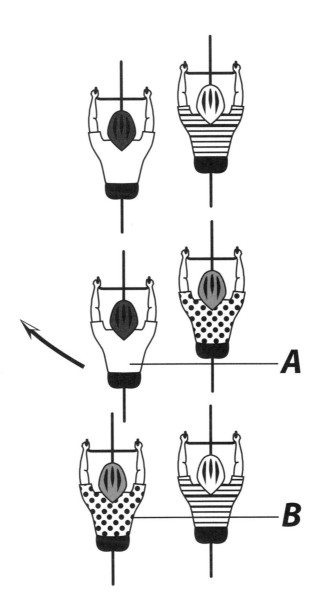

Diagram 12.2: Rider A could easily take out rider B's front wheel with a quick move to the left.

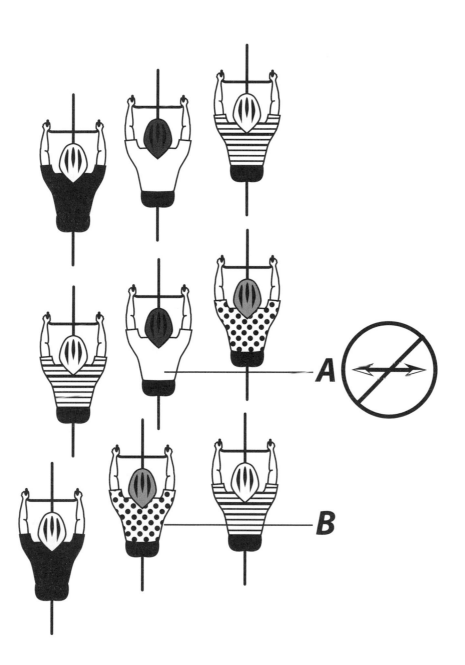

Diagram 12.3: In a tight pack rider A cannot move to the right or the left. Rider B is safe.

you're there. That should be all that's necessary. If you recognize someone as a particularly bad bike handler, it's best to avoid overlapping his wheel. He might have very little regard and veer off into you.

Inside a tightly knit peloton, a lot of racers are going to have overlapped wheels. This isn't generally a problem, because when everyone is sandwiched together (see Diagram 12.3) no one can move quickly to one side or the other.

EVASIVE ACTIONS

It is possible to take some evasive action should someone swerve into your wheel, but prevention is still your best defense. Having your front wheel hit is potentially so dangerous that evasion may have to be a last-ditch effort.

Just as it is possible to throw your bike forward in a sprint, you can pull your bike backward. This is what you should attempt when a wheel swerves into your front wheel—jerk back on your handlebars, pulling your bike underneath you as you throw your weight forward (see Diagram 12.4). This brings your bike several inches backward in relation to the rear wheel of the racer in front of you. Hopefully it is enough to get you out of trouble. Unfortunately, this quick movement may cause problems for the racers behind you. Still it is better than causing a pileup after falling over the wheel.

Another possible evasive action is to lean your bike sharply away from the rear wheel that's just hit your front

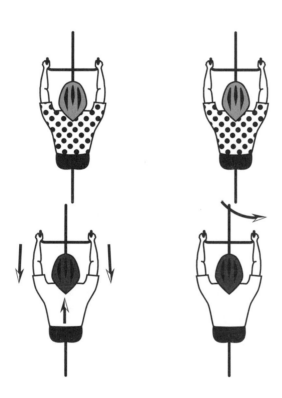

Diagram 12.4: Pulling the bike backward

Diagram 12.5: Leaning the bike away from the rear wheel

wheel. This is difficult, because you must turn the bike in the opposite direction to which you are leaning (see Diagram 12.5). The bike, if you've reacted soon enough, turns away from the rear wheel that almost tripped you up.

These two techniques can be combined to some extent. It all comes down to bike handling. These techniques can also be practiced with a training partner in your grass field. It's not necessary for you to actually hit the rear wheel in front of you. Just get close enough to the rear wheel to see what effect your actions have and how to move out of danger.

BRAKING DRILL

I once overheard a comment from a racer that still sticks with me, even though I know (I hope!) he was joking.

"Brakes?" he asked "Who wants to use the brakes on your bike? I want to go fast. I don't want to slow down."

A humorous comment; but, of course, we all have to use our brakes now and again. Whether for cornering or avoiding a crash, you should know how to use the bike's brakes in extreme situations. By knowing how and when to brake, you can actually go faster.

Take the example of going into a corner. Let's say you can approach a particular corner at 32 mph, but the fastest you can possibly negotiate it is at just 26 mph. The later you initiate your braking sequence before the corner, the sooner you can exit coming out of the corner.

Diagram 12.6: It is necessary to shift your body weight when hitting the brakes hard.

Before starting a few drills, it's important to understand some of the dynamics of braking to know how the bike handles and how you will have to handle the bike.

If the front brake is locked, you will catapult over the handlebars. If the rear brake is locked, the rear wheel will lose traction and you'll skid. In situations where the brakes are applied very hard, the rear wheel "lightens." Locking the rear wheel and skidding isn't the fastest way to slow down. Obviously locking the front wheel is not the best method, either. In both cases, the rear wheel has a tendency to lose traction by either skidding or lightening up. Therefore, when hitting the brakes hard, slide your body weight aft to keep traction and on the ground (see Diagram 12.6).

Braking drills are designed to give you a better feel for how your bike handles when trying to stop in extreme situations. While these drills should be started on grass for safety reasons, the only way to really get a feel for how your bike and brakes handle when stressed is to test them on smooth pavement.

Start off on a grassy field to see just when, how, or even if your brakes grab. If you have a little hill to work with, come off the hill to build up some speed. Pick out a mark on the field to start your braking. When you reach the mark, jam on the rear brake. Continue this a few times until you find the maximum braking pressure you can apply without skidding. Since this drill is on grass, you'll lose traction sooner than you would on pavement.

For the front brake drill use the same hill or field and marker, but start off by applying only a small amount of pressure on the brakes. Continue to increase the pressure until you start to feel the rear wheel "lighten."

After getting comfortable with these brake drills on a field, move to a smooth, clean, and above all, deserted road or parking lot to get a better feel for how your bike and brakes respond on pavement. Start off by applying less brake and then increasing it fractionally until you reach the limit where you lose traction.

Of course, the best braking is when you use both front and rear at the same time. It is still necessary to slide to the back of the saddle, or even off the back of the saddle in extreme braking circumstances.

The result of all of these drills will be more control in braking. You should feel comfortable when hitting the brakes hard, either to negotiate a corner or to avoid a crash.

ANOTHER WORD OF CAUTION

Not all of your wheels may handle the same way when braking extremely hard. Changing rims will change the "feel" of your bike. This has to do with the shape and material the rims are made from. Of course, the condition of the rim can affect braking as well. A little flat spot in a rim, caused from hitting a pothole or rock, can cause the brake to grab unexpectedly.

A little tire glue on the rim can also cause a wheel to brake inconsistently. Get used to the feel of your race wheels.

Of course the same rule applies to brakes as well. Different brake systems feel completely different. Some stop you much quicker than others. I was quite comfortable with a certain company's brakes from a year of training and racing. Then, our team changed component companies. The first day out on my new bike, I was zooming up on a lane of traffic stopped at a light. I reached for the brake levers and started squeezing at the appropriate moment. The driver in the pickup truck was quite startled when he heard a loud thud on his back bumper. It suddenly became apparent to me (and to him) that I was going to have to learn the feel of braking again.

Final Word

None of these are remedial skills. These drills will help you learn to handle your bike better and more safely and you need to keep them honed. Try to devote a regular amount of time to doing these basic drills each week, whether it's a full 30-minute session in a field with the sole purpose of working on handling or just 3 or 4 minutes of spare time while waiting for a training partner to show up for a ride. It will all add up to a small investment of time that can literally save your skin.

Mental Training

Think about it for a moment. There are several hundred professional racers in the world who dedicate themselves 100 percent to their livelihood. They would spend 10 hours a day or more training on the bike, if that is what it would take to be better than the next guy. But darn it . . . you can't train 10 hours a day for very long before your body would collapse from exhaustion.

There are physical limitations that keep us from simply stacking on more and more miles and having it benefit. In fact, there is considerable data to indicate that training has to be done in moderation for it to be of value. So where does that leave the dedicated pro? Now there are several hundred professional racers who have reached a level of fitness that can hardly be topped. There is a crowded field of competitors who are all at about the same level. There is almost always a rider or two who does rise above the rest with extraordinary talents like LeMond, Hinault, or Armstrong. These riders are anomalies.

What separates the tight field of competitors are their tactics, a little bit of luck, and their desire to win. Over the course of a season, we have to assume that good ol' luck will eventually be dealt evenly to all. Tactics we learn and apply. There are those riders who are better at applying tactics than others, but still most professionals have become masters at tactical cycling. The only other thing that separates the rider who wins from the rest of the pack is desire.

Desire is a rather abstract concept. Either you have it or you don't. It's an emotional state brought on by mental process. So what do we do to distinguish ourselves from the tightly packed field of elite athletes? What can we do since we're already training at our absolute optimum? What other legal and ethically acceptable methods can we employ to give ourselves the little edge that gives a significant advantage at the elite level? We can work on that emotional state and on the mental process.

If heart rate training was the exercise discovery of the 1980s and power training the discovery of the 1990s, perhaps mental training will be the wave of this new millennium. When we have reached nearly the edge of the physical barrier, our pursuit for perfection has to now focus inward on the mind.

A day's mileage and intervals could be complemented sitting quietly for half an hour of purely mental exercise. Frequently you hear athletes of all sports admit that, at the elite level, competition win is 10 percent physical and 90 percent mental. This simply means that the athlete who won did so not on physical strength—so many of the riders are all at the same level of fitness—but on mental toughness. Now, doesn't it seem odd that if the mental aspect of racing is so critical why so few people take the time to exercise the mind in a beneficial manner?

Programming the Control System

The mind is like a computer. Maybe you've heard the computer expression: "GIGO," which translates to Garbage In, Garbage Out. If you feed junk programming into a computer, the results will also be junk. If you keep telling yourself that you can't do something, pretty soon you'll have convinced yourself. In cycling, you might end up worrying about a climb in an upcoming race. You tell yourself, "I can't make it up that climb with the pack. I can't make it up that . . . I just can't!" Rather than simply thinking about it, you wind up making an affirmation that you won't succeed. Like a computer, you end up feeding garbage into your mind. Since the mind doesn't know the difference between your worrying and you actually stating fact . . . the mind understands it as fact.

Bicycle racing and life are filled with challenges like 5-mile climbs, crowded field sprints, deadlines, and down payments. If you let worrying consume your thoughts and turn it into a negative affirmation, you'll struggle a lot harder. On the other side of the fence are those individuals who use the same power of the mind for their benefit.

One summer I was a member of a team aiming for the national title in the 100-km team time trial. The four of us trained together for nearly a month. We were isolated in the mountains with no distractions. The training was very tough. None of us had much experience at the event, and we knew we would be racing against the defending national champions. I wanted to make sure I was doing everything possible to ensure our success. It was a perfect opportunity to do some experimenting of my own with mental training.

Each afternoon, when we had returned from our workouts, I would lie down for some rest. Rather than daydreaming—or worse, *worrying* about the event—I would think positively about the approaching race. I would relax for a few moments, let my thoughts settle, and then I would think intensely about the race coming up, always in a positive manner. I would run the entire race through my mind from start to finish to climbing onto the victory podium, just the way I wanted it to happen. I would live the event—resulting in a win—over and over in my mind. I would imagine how my legs would feel after each pull; sore, but strong. I would preview in my mind the feeling of my legs recovering before I reached the front to take another pull. I imagined shifting gears. I imagined the sweat rolling down my arms. I pulled the national champion's jersey on over my head more than twenty times in this powerful daydream before I actually did it in person.

After the success with those national championships, I used the same technique on the way to several major victories, including my win at the 1986 USPRO Championship. The way I incorporated this mental training really can't be done for every weekend criterium (it *does* take a lot of energy), but the techniques can be applied for everyday life. You are what you eat and you become what you think of yourself. Use positive thinking in all facets of your life for better results. It works!

The old Spenco 500 was another good example of the power of positive thinking. I was talked into doing the race by a teammate. He told me all about what the event had been like the year before. We trained for about a month specifically for the 500-mile race. There was no way I was going to ride 500 miles without having clear intentions of winning. I knew it would be tough and I knew that when it came right down to it, the race would be won in the mind of the competitors and not on the road. I was a little surprised when we showed up the night before the race and there were eighty very good racers and even a few European professionals thrown in for good measure. We were also a little surprised by the weather. Instead of the hot, sunny Texas weather everyone was expecting, it was cold and overcast.

Five hours into the race—right when it started to get dark—it started to rain. Imagine racing for 24 hours and having half of them in the dark, in the rain, and with temperatures that didn't rise above 45 degrees. If a rider started to dwell on the conditions, he would mentally talk himself out of the race. That's what a lot of the riders did.

But for me, going into the race, I knew that I could never even *think* about quitting. NEVER! When I went over and over the race in my head the weeks before, quitting was just never an option. In the race, I simply didn't entertain that thought. And it never entered my mind . . . all the way through the 500 miles and that last walk up to the top of the podium.

TRANSCENDENTAL MEDITATION (TM)

Long before the 100-km training camp, I understood the power of the mind. When I was first getting serious about bicycle racing, I heard about a simple, effortless mental technique whereby one could experience profound rest and relaxation. The technique, Transcendental Meditation, could give me an added advantage over my competitors. I figured I could train that much harder if I could get that much deeper rest. I quickly learned the technique from a certified instructor and started enjoying the benefits. If there is one thing I've done that has made the most difference in my racing career and personal life (and I sincerely mean this), it was learning TM.

What started out as a way to get some extra rest has turned out to be a technique of ongoing positive influence and beneficial results. There are volumes of scientific literature documenting the clinical benefits of TM for athletes and others. Let's just say I've been pleased enough with the results to still want to find time to meditate every day.

There are numerous popular books on mental toughness training, the power of positive thinking, and Transcendental Meditation. Pick one up and start exploring the possibilities. You'll be a pioneer into the next training discovery.

Keeping a Training and Racing Diary

THE BASICS

A training diary is different from a yearly training plan. The yearly plan is just that—a plan for you to get from the present to the future and arrive there in shape to realize your goals. A training diary is a detailed record of exactly what you did during the day that is related to your training and racing. Keeping a diary is a helpful addition to your yearly training plan. While the training plan helps you look ahead, the training diary is for looking back. When you hit a real stride in your form or bog down in racing, the training diary is a valuable key to discovering the causes. From there you can avoid replicating them. Training should not be a "hit or miss" proposition, and your detailed diary brings some science into the method.

There are a lot of great digital training diary options out there from software and Web sites that record a lot of data. Some of these are quite sophisticated in terms of what they capture and can allow you to review. While I like a lot of these, I still also like to keep a plain old notebook for writing down some notes, racecourse diagrams, and other things that are a pain to record on a computer.

For eight years I used the exact same type of book as a training diary. It has all the necessary spots for recording data and plenty of room to write about each ride and race. The hardbound *Cash Account Book* I like is available in most office supply stores. The book is small and light, yet durable enough for traveling. It's an ideal diary. There's a column for the date, your weight, pulse rate, pulse rate difference, and training mileage. Below all of that information, I write briefly about the training and workouts I did for the day and any other pertinent information.

The most difficult part about a training diary or training plan is keeping up with it every day. I keep my training diary on a bedside table, so I can write in it first thing in the morning or at night before I go to sleep. The current month's training plan can be stuck in the book for quick reference each morning.

POST-RACE ANALYSIS

Perhaps one of the more important entries you can make into this training diary is after a race. With the event fresh in your mind, detail the race. Write down all that happened and what you saw. Write in what mistakes you made or saw during the race. Note data like race week, because races are usually held on the weekend. If your sights aren't firmly set on something on the horizon, you'll probably taper a bit for each weekend's race. Now you can plan to train through some events, or use the events as training themselves.

To start filling in your training plan, work backward from the most important dates. The day before is 1, two days before 2, and so on. On a separate sheet of paper, list all of the basic types of workouts that you want to do or need to do throughout the year. Remember, quite often the workouts we *need* to do are the ones we avoid. This list should have specific types of workouts; it can be fairly detailed. Don't forget easy workouts and rides, too. Now, go back to the training plan calendar and start to fill in all the dates, working from the most important backward up until next week (or tomorrow).

As you fill in the workouts, you might suddenly realize that there's now a tangible connection from your desire in the future to the present. Don't be surprised if you suddenly find the need to get on your bike and ride.

Your training dairy should have sufficient information to record and recall each day's training, the gears you used on particular climbs or in the sprint, amount of food you ate, and so on. You'll have a record to look back at for reference. In the case of using a gear on a climb, the information can be critical to your success if you ride the same course next year.

Write down how you felt during the race. There's nothing better than honest analysis of your physical state to help determine where your training should go. This analysis should flush out your weak points and give you something to work on in training. And everyone has areas they can improve on! Try to remember and note how you felt emotionally during the race as well. Note how you responded mentally to the various aspects of the race. Did you back off too much in the corners when someone chopped you? How did you respond when everyone started fighting for position at the finish? Were you riding in the front of the pack or were you hanging on?

Writing down the mistakes you've made brings them into full light for you to examine. If you're determined, you'll rarely make the same mistake twice, once you've fully documented it to yourself. Recording everything else you saw should make you a wiser racer by learning from other racers' mistakes.

FINAL WORD

As with any endeavor, I come to the end of this book and I still feel like there is more to tell you. There has to be something—even if it's glaringly obvious—that I can make a point of saying so that your racing experience becomes even more successful. But the key here, and what I hope I've conveyed over the course of these pages, is that bike racing is an elegant and beautifully tactical sport. These ideas are really just the start. You will discover that one tactic or move can be combined with others and morphed to appear completely different. As I said when I began this project with my old *Pro Form Racing* newsletters, my ultimate goal is to help other riders avoid common mistakes, ride better, and race smarter.

The rules established in this book can be summed up in just a few words. To be consistently successful in bicycle racing, you need to *think*, *plan*, and *act*; but now I am going to add another component—*review*. It will be from introspection or team discussion following a race that all of this will start to really come together. If you are smart, you will never stop learning!

Bicycle racing is a thinking man's sport. It's a three-dimensional, high-speed chess game, sometimes involving hundreds of pieces on the board. From tactics to training schedules, you succeed in this sport only with a *combination* of physical and mental fortitude. To be a success on the road, a rider has to make a serious commitment to the sport. The foundation of that success is training, but to take full advantage of whatever fitness you have attained, you need to think like a tactician.

I hope now that armed a deeper appreciation of the tactical nature of the sport, you will invariably begin to see races through a different set of eyes. Remember and learn from your mistakes and build on your successes. I believe you will be pleasantly surprised.

Good luck,
Thomas

INDEX

Note: Page numbers in italics refer to diagrams.

About the Authors

Thomas Prehn has been involved with cycling since he took up the sport in the early 1970s. Over the course of a long career as an amateur and professional cyclist, he won the 1986 USPRO road championship, and is one of the few cyclists to have finished all thirteen editions of the Red Zinger/Coors Classic. A consistent top finisher in U.S. national championship races throughout his career, Prehn was also a member of the winning U.S. national time trial team in 1982.

Prehn currently lives in Boulder, Colorado where he is the director of CatEye Service & Research Center and president of his own consumer research and consulting firm, Boulder Sports Research. He is also the current vice president of the Bicycle Products Suppliers Association.

With his two full time jobs, and a family, Prehn still likes to mix it up at the weekend races. He now races with the intensity that most people go to garage sales. He can be reached at Thomas@bicycleresearch.com.

Charles Pelkey is a former amateur bike racer, and has enjoyed a long and varied media career—working as a political reporter, a U.S. senate press secretary, and even a late-night jazz disc jockey. He has been the technical editor of *VeloNews* since 1994, and lives in Golden, Colorado with his wife Diana Denison and their children Philip and Annika.